LIGHTING
the
LAMP

The Theosophical Publishing House
P.O. Box 270
Wheaton, IL 60189-0270

A publication of the Theosophical Publishing House,
a department of the Theosophical Society in America.

Library of Congress Cataloging-in-Publication Data

Woll, Alfred.
    Lighting the lamp : an approach to the Tibetan path /
Alfred Woll.
      p. cm.
    "Quest books."
    ISBN 0-8356-0686-4 (pbk.) : $12.00
    1. Spiritual life — Buddhism.   2. Buddhism — China — Tibet —
Doctrines.   I. Title.
BQ7815.W65   1992
294.3′923 — dc20   92-50144
                                                      CIP

9 8 7 6 5 4 3 2 1 * 92 93 94 95 96 97 98 99

This edition is printed on acid-free paper that meets the
American National Standards Institute Z39.48 Standard

Printed in the United States of America by Versa Press

If the darkness that hides the basis of right and wrong
Is not illuminated by the lamp of true learning,
You cannot know even the path; not to speak of
Entrance into the supreme city of liberation!
                                        —Tsongkhapa

Contents

Foreword

I first met Alfred Woll while on a teaching tour in
Malaysia in 1984. He and four or five young Germans
were traveling around Asia after completing a meditation
course in Thailand. Alfred's appearance was typical of
the Western hippies seen throughout Asia—some of his
hair was twisted into a thin long braid, and his jacket
was covered with embroidery. But his attitude set him
apart; he was serious and intent, always questioning
deeply and seeking to further his understanding.

Alfred's interest in Buddhism continued to grow, and
he somehow managed to attach himself to the group
traveling with me. The Malaysians who were my hosts
are always so hospitable. They took Alfred in, offering
him meals and places to stay. As the tour was coming to
an end and I was preparing to leave, Alfred and another
young man approached me saying that they planned to
extend their stay in Asia and do a meditation retreat.
They requested my advice, and I suggested subjects for
their meditation.

When I met Alfred again a few years later in Europe,
he had clearly undergone a tremendous change. His
mind had become more smooth and settled, and his
compassion had increased considerably. Though he still
questioned deeply and was always seeking clarification,
his commitment to spiritual practice had grown quite
stable.

Since that time Alfred has visited me several times in
the United States and in Europe. For the last year or so,
he has been living in The Netherlands with a group of
my students and helping them with their study and

a culture much different from their own. Encouraged by my kind teacher Gelek Rinpoche, I began to work on the problem by comparing my experiences with those of other teachers in the West and those of senior dharma students. Out of these discussions, I developed a curriculum for the students of Jewel Heart/Holland to offer a basic program to help new and prospective dharma students set the priorities necessary to begin to change their lives.

The material presented in this book is based on a program of lectures and meditation instruction I gave in Holland in 1991. The dharma topics examined in Part I give an overview of the Buddhist path and set the stage for actual practice. The meditation exercises suggested in Part II explore the nature of the mind and help develop the mindfulness required for further spiritual development. The appendix summarizes the result of a survey among a group of senior American dharma students who have been engaged in practicing the meditations suggested in this book.

I dedicate any benefit derived from this work to all living beings. May they find the happiness they seek.

Alfred Woll
Nijmegen, Holland
March, 1992

Acknowledgments

I am most grateful to my teacher Gelek Rinpoche who over the years has unceasingly answered my questions and guided me along the path. I would also like to thank all the friends in America and Holland who shared their experiences with me and gave me their suggestions and assistance. I am especially grateful to Brenda Rosen, who was of essential help in editing the manuscript, improving my poor English with great skill and care and making many valuable contributions to the content and form of presentation. I would also like to thank Aura Glaser for her assistance and checking of the final draft, Madonna Gauding for her fine illustrations, and the staff of the Theosophical Publishing House for producing this work.

The Precious Parasol gives protection from all evil.

PART I
Dharma

1

Consume-Orientation or Self-Evolvement

When we take a moment to observe, we see people around us engaging in all kinds of activities. Everyone is rushing from here to there, talking on the phone, arguing with a neighbor, meeting a friend, shopping for groceries or clothes, working in an office or in a store. Even riding a bicycle or hanging out on the beach is an activity. Noticing all this busyness, we might ask ourselves: Why do we do all this? What is the purpose of our wide variety of actions and reactions? If we think carefully and trace our motivation back to the root, we will discover a simple answer. We and all the other busy people in the world are seeking happiness and trying to avoid unpleasantness or suffering.

We all want happiness—not only human beings but animals as well. In pursuit of this happiness, we are constantly in motion, active and restless, loving and fighting. If all beings want only happiness, and if we engage in countless activities to secure happiness, why do we so often experience misery, problems, and a pervasive sense of discontent? Perhaps we don't know how to be happy, or even know what real, lasting happiness feels like.

People clearly *think* they know what happiness is. For one person, happiness might seem to be a successful

business; for another, it is a new spouse or partner; a
third might seek happiness in artistic or creative work.
Still others seek happiness through one spiritual path
or another, or through making a lot of money on the
market, or by winning fame, influence, or political
power. But when we have achieved one of these goals,
do we also achieve lasting happiness? Sometimes, for a
short while, we seem happy. Eventually, however, the
old dissatisfied feeling comes back, and we restlessly
seek more of what we have or something different to
make us happy.

Moreover, our busy daily lives seldom give us a
chance to take stock of what we want or where we are
going. The rush starts as we jump out of bed to shower
and dress for work. Our breakfast is often a hurried bite
while we glance at the paper, listen to the radio or
television, and talk to our spouse or housemate about all
the things we have to do that day. Then we battle traffic
or jostle our way through a crowded bus or train to get
to work, where our desk is piled high with tasks.
For relief, we may window-shop at lunch or read a
magazine, brimming with advertisements urging us to
buy this or that. When we get home, our family also has
needs—the children need help with their homework, or
we have promised to take them to a movie, a restaurant,
or a sports event. On a good day, there is no place to
go, and we collapse in front of the TV because we are so
tired. Don't we all know days like this?

No wonder our minds become overburdened. Bom-
barded constantly with stimulation, demands, information, and desires from outside and from within, we lose
our steadiness and balance. In this tense and aggressive
state, little things cause conflicts with people around us.
Underlying the routine of our lives is a deep well of
dissatisfaction. We feel we are missing something, but
what?

Given the busyness of our lives, this question seems

almost impossible to answer. Since our minds are so overloaded with daily impressions, our thoughts are never stilled long enough for us to really experience our feelings and see what it is we are missing. Our discontent becomes just another little boat pitching up and down in the stormy ocean of the mind. We don't know where our dissatisfaction comes from or where it is leading us. We simply feel its pervasive quality underlying all that we do or think.

When we become aware of our dissatisfaction, we try to scratch the itch. Every radio, TV, or billboard advertisement cleverly tells us how to buy satisfaction and happiness: What you need is a new car, a bigger house, a vacation in Hawaii, a fine meal in a restaurant, a big cream cake. In this wealthy country, most of us can certainly get all the goodies we wish for. But when we get the house or the car or the cake, what happens? How long does the satisfaction last? How long before we start to pine for the next vacation, the next shopping spree? Sometimes we do realize the temporary quality of our satisfactions. When this happens, we often get depressed and feel helpless, though we don't know exactly what is wrong. Since I have all these things, we say to ourselves, why am I not happy?

When this question arises, we must intervene to break the pattern. If we can for a moment step outside the vicious cycle, sit back quietly, observe ourselves, and analyze our situation fairly, we may realize that we, like the majority of people in the world, have been seeking happiness through outer objects and conditions. We have been seeking lovers and friends to stave off loneliness and to make up for our own insufficiencies. We have been seeking amusement, excitement, and stimulation in a futile attempt to cover up or escape from our own boredom and to still our basic dissatisfaction.

This attitude of seeking happiness through external things can be called *consume-orientation*. This term means

that one tries to find security through possessing and
having, and to find happiness and joy through acquiring
and consuming. Consume-orientation is propagated
everywhere in Western society. We have grown up with
this attitude, and most of us accept it without question.

However, it's not difficult to puncture the consume-
orientation bubble. We have only to look around us at
the frightening statistics of drug addiction and crime,
suicide and mental illness. If material wealth truly guar-
antees happiness, why are so many of us so miserable?
When we look more closely, we see how the mechanism
of consume-orientation really works. In essence, the
more one has, the more one wants. Our desires only get
bigger. Whatever we need, we need again and again, or
we need more, or we need something better. Seeking
happiness through consume-orientation is like trying to
reach the horizon. No matter how far we travel, no
matter how much we speed up or run, the horizon
always remains in the far distance, leaving us stuck in
the dissatisfaction of where we are.

For most of us, consume-orientation underlies and
motivates everything we do. Because we feel fearful and
insecure, we accumulate wealth to get us through bad
times and buy insurance to protect us against calamities.
Because we feel inferior, we acquire titles, status, and
prestigious possessions. Because we feel bored and
dissatisfied, we entertain ourselves through exciting relationships and other sensual pleasures. When we feel
upset and depressed, we distract ourselves by indulging
in addictions to alcohol, food, or drugs.

Each of these patterns of activity is really a desperate
attempt to heal painful feelings of inner emptiness by
applying a remedy from outside. Once we have
recognized this pattern through careful observation and
analysis, we may come to the conclusion that actions
motivated by consume-orientation can never bring us
lasting happiness. The pervasive feeling that we lack

something, that we are incomplete, isolated, and separated, can never be remedied fully by external objects or experiences.

As we think further, we realize that because all external things and experiences are by their very nature perishable, unreliable, and uncertain, they are destined to change and decay and can never give us real security. We also come to see that if we try to overcome feelings of inferiority by achieving a prestigious title, a mansion, and a Mercedes, we are hoping that glittering decorations will uplift our own value or deceive others about the real issue. Deep inside, we still feel small and inferior. Similarly, our habitual response to boredom, dissatisfaction, and unwanted emotions is to try to cover up or mask these symptoms of inescapable discontent. To be consume-oriented seems clearly to be heading in the wrong direction. But what other way is there to solve our existential problems?

The Motivation of Self-Evolvement

The opposite of consume-orientation, with its focus on external objects, is *self-evolvement*, which is focused on the development of one's own personality or inner nature. Self-evolvement leads to a different state of being rather than a different collection of things. Instead of surrounding ourselves with material things and identifying with them as in consume-orientation, we develop a presence within us and become that which we imagine. The meditations described in Part II of this book help us begin this process. In consume-orientation we often superimpose projected images on ourselves, such as the image of being strong and courageous, under which we hide our sense of weakness or fear. Self-evolvement, on the other hand, is a way of becoming authentic. What we say and do is the same as what we think and feel, which is the same as what we are. Consider, for exam-

ple, a person like Gandhi or Mother Teresa. Such men
and women may possess only a handful of material
things, but they are nevertheless rich with wisdom and
authentic presence. They are impressive for what they
are, rather than for what they have. They radiate such
warmth, love, and care, such joy and inner peace, that
everyone who comes in contact with them is touched.

Self-evolvement is a freeing process which ripens our
inner potential by increasing our positive qualities. As
we become one with these qualities, we become more
and more real. The path of self-evolvement creates
balance and harmony within ourselves, thus freeing us
from the compulsions caused by our fears and addictions. Even when we face threatening or painful outer
circumstances, a condition of self-evolvement allows us
to remain in a state of equanimity, allowing changing
conditions to flow over us without arousing strong feelings of attachment and aversion. Who would not want
the strength to keep a balanced, loving mind in whatever situation he or she encounters? Who would not
want the ability to remain always in a state of inner
peace and contentment?

The first step in achieving such a state is to look
inside. We must realize who we are by becoming aware
of our thoughts, attitudes, fears, and wishes. Once we
know ourselves, we can begin to make friends with
ourselves and accept even those parts of our personality
we have denied or tried to cover up. Instead of disap-
proving of or even hating ourselves, we begin to feel
compassion for our own suffering and embrace our
whole being. In so doing, we begin to understand our
habitual patterns of acting and reacting and see how our
activities and motivations are interrelated. When we
become grounded in ourselves, we can avoid following
fantasies and projections that lead inevitably to disappointment, conflict, and pain. Through such introspection, we come to recognize and accept our potential for

higher evolution, and as we start to develop this potential, we gain deeper understanding of ourselves and of the functioning of the world outside. This understanding is the basis of wisdom, which frees us from the ever-tightening noose of negative habitual patterns and gives us the freedom to choose actions that develop our positive potential.

When we hear such glowing scenarios of how we can change, many of us no doubt think, "But this is how I am. This is my character. I have always been like this. How can I change myself totally? How can I be other than what I am right now?" This negative estimation of our potential blocks positive development. Let us look more closely at this feeling that we cannot change.

What we call personality is actually a habitual way of thinking, acting, and reacting. If we analyze ourselves carefully, we will find that the "character" we are so sure we cannot change is nothing more than a set of mental attitudes and behavior patterns which we have acquired through a process of learning. We are the way we are because we have been conditioned to act and react a certain way by the sum total of our past experiences. All that we have done and all that we have encountered formed our present personality. But we are constantly encountering new situations and new experiences, and our character and personality are continuously changing. Every new experience that we have and any small change that we undergo makes it more likely that we will form new patterns and develop new ways of acting. Every repetition of an action reinforces that habit and makes it more likely that we will perform the action again.

With the realization that our personality is formed by causes and conditions and is, therefore, a dependent process which keeps on changing, it becomes clear that the future is up to us. What we become depends on the new imprints we make on our mindstream: what negative

habits we reduce and what positive habits we reinforce
and cultivate. If we really want change, then improvement is possible. Moreover, not only can we change
ourselves, but the world around us can also lose its
unpleasant appearance. We assume that the world and
the beings in it are in reality exactly as they appear to
us, and we believe that qualities and attributes exist
within the object from its own side. But do they?

Consider the example of John, a truckdriver. Every
Monday when John climbs into his truck and begins
his week-long run, he experiences a familiar sense of
despair. To John, the greasy truck cab is a moving
prison, a box in which he moves along a dusty road for
five days, until the weekend when he can see his family
again. To John, the truck is an object of misery. However, he has a young son. When John allows his son to
sit behind the wheel of the truck, the boy is in a state
of bliss. To the son, the truck cab is a lofty throne. The
son hopes that when he is older he can become a truckdriver like his father. To him, his father's big truck is an
object of highest pleasure.

Which view of the truck is the real one? In fact, the
truck itself is neither an object of pleasure nor an object
of misery. Such perceptions are based on the mental
attitude of the perceiving individual. From its side, the
truck is a neutral object. The relative perspective of a
subjective perceiver actually determines what is felt
toward an object. The same is true for any other object,
person, or situation. Our perception of a person as a
friend, enemy, or stranger depends on our viewpoint.
Given this, we begin to understand that our viewpoint is
a relative component which can be changed volitionally,
enabling us to view and experience things in a new way.
If we assume a different viewpoint, the "unpleasantness" of an object can be made to disappear. Eventually,
everything we encounter in life can become a source of
joy. Having developed such deep awareness, it is possi-

ble to perceive in addition to the relative view of objects, their absolute nature—their suchness—which recognizes objects for just what they are.

Let's return for a moment to John the truckdriver. Twenty years have passed, and John has retired. Hanging in John's den are many photographs of his truck and its old rusty license plates. When he is in the mood, John speaks nostalgically about the wonderful adventures he had driving his truck from Canada to Mexico. John's son is now finishing college. He is planning to be a teacher. Sometimes he feels sorry for his father and for the boring and lonely job he had as a truckdriver. Trucks no longer appeal to him.

Thus in time and in accordance with circumstances, views can change, and the world around us and everything in it can acquire a new appearance. Even painful and difficult situations and individuals can become things we love and care for. When we adopt the attitude of self-evolvement, with its inevitable loosening of our fixed attitudes and projections, we can come to realize that the world and our lives can be exactly as we make them. As we develop the wisdom of seeing things for what they are, we see more clearly who we are and how we are interlinked with every other being. When this happens, our feelings of isolation and separation will dissolve, and we will open to a new sense of warmth, love, and caring for others and for ourselves.

*The White Conch Shell Horn, its coils spiralling to the
right, proclaims the fame of the saints.*

2

The Relevance of the
Buddha's Life Story

The life story of the Buddha is known to most of us. Hearing its familiar details, we might be moved by the Buddha's experiences and achievements, but not very often do we see the deeper messages which lie within the beautiful story of a prince's life journey twenty-five hundred years ago. What, we may ask, does the Buddha's search and realization have to do with the problems and questions of an ordinary person living in the West in the twentieth century? Clearly the significance of the Buddha's story does not lie in the historical facts. These are hard to prove and difficult to distinguish from the colorful embellishments added later by the Buddha's devotees. Rather the significance of this biography lies in its illustration of the method by which any person can resolve the basic problems of human life. In this simple story is a message not bound to any time or culture but to human existence as a whole.

Before examining the significance of the story, let us review its details. In the sixth century B.C. the social structure of India was dominated by the Hindu caste system. The Brahmans, the highest and best-educated caste, held both spiritual and temporal power. This concentration of priestly and worldly authority within one group often led to oppression of the lower castes. The

religious underpinnings of this system, the Vedas and
Hinduism, supported the theory that class differences
were determined by karma, the natural law of cause and
effect. If a person followed the right livelihood and kept
pure ethics, he or she could achieve rebirth in a higher
caste in the next life. The aim of a spiritual person was
to reach higher and higher levels through repeated incarnation until finally attaining freedom from the circle of
rebirth and unification with the universal soul from
which everything originated. Many Hindus and followers
of other minor religious sects led lives of ascetic practice
in an effort to speed up the process of self-liberation.
Though the prevailing system was accepted by all, many
in the lower castes were discontented with its inequities.

Into this milieu in a small kingdom on the plains of
northern India, Prince Siddhartha Gautama was born to
King Shuddhodana and Queen Maya. Before the birth,
the queen had several auspicious dreams about the child
growing in her womb, and at Siddhartha's birth, rain-
bows appeared in the sky. It was prophesied that if the
prince chose to lead a worldly life, he would become a
universal monarch, but if he turned away from a political
career and followed a spiritual life, he would become a
great savior.

Soon after giving birth, the queen died. Siddhartha's
father was anxious for his son to succeed him as king.
He arranged for the finest tutors to teach the boy to read
and write, to excel in every sort of game and sport, and
to appreciate the sciences and the arts. He surrounded
Siddhartha with all the luxuries and splendors of the
royal court: festivity, women, music, food, and dance.
To protect his son from experiencing the misery of the
world, the king forbade him to leave the palace. At six-
teen, Siddhartha was married to the lovely Gopa.

For twelve years, Siddhartha lived in magnificence
and pleasure. Gopa bore him a son named Rahula. Yet
despite the worldly riches of his life within the palace

walls, Sidhartha was restless and dissatisfied. He left the palace confines three times with his charioteer to venture into the world. On his first journey, he saw an old man; on his second, a sick man; and on his third, a corpse. These sights shocked Siddhartha into the realization that he too, like all men and women, was subject to old age, sickness, and death. Venturing from the palace a fourth time, Siddhartha encountered a wandering mendicant who had left his family to live a life of simplicity and introspection in an attempt to find freedom and inner peace. Siddhartha resolved to do likewise.

Returning to the palace, Siddhartha took leave of his father, who tried unsuccessfully to convince him to stay. Then Siddhartha crossed to the women's chamber to bid farewell to his wife. The female servants, musicians, and dancers had all fallen asleep, lying untidily on the ground. As he gazed at his sleeping wife, her physical body, which had only yesterday appeared so attractive, now seemed ugly to Siddhartha, and he recognized the impermanence of all sensory pleasures. Ordering his servant to prepare horses, Siddhartha left the palace that evening. After riding through the night, Siddhartha dismounted. He laid aside his royal garments and jewels, and with his sword cut off his hair. He set off, barefoot and clad in a simple garment, to seek liberation—release from the never-ending cycle of birth, death, and rebirth.

For a year, Siddhartha traveled through the Indian countryside, learning from various spiritual teachers. His first teacher told him that the phenomena of the physical world are nonexistent. Siddhartha refuted this theory and continued his search. A second teacher taught him a meditation to reach a state of neither perception nor nonperception. But Siddhartha saw that this method also was not sufficient to attain liberation. After studying and mastering the methods of spiritual training practiced by the greatest religious teachers of his day, Siddhartha retreated to the woods with five other ascetics to practice

an austere life of fasting and meditation. For six agoniz-
ing years, Siddhartha sought realization through self-
denial. His body became weak and emaciated. Finally he
understood that torturing the body was not the way to
escape cyclic existence.

Siddhartha then washed himself in a nearby river,
wrapped himself in a clean garment, and ate a meal of
sweet milk rice prepared by a young woman. Then he
sat down under a bodhi tree with the intention not to
arise until he had found the way to transcend the sufferings of old age, sickness, and death. He was confronted
by many internal and external forces and temptations,
but his meditative concentration was not disturbed. At
the first light of dawn of the full moon of the fourth
lunar month, Siddhartha achieved paranormal perception. He saw his previous lives and those of all other
sentient beings. He saw that all beings who are born
into cyclic existence are bound to suffer. Ignorant of the
workings of karma and attached to the phenomena of
the world which they perceive as existing inherently,
beings act in such ways as to create the karma that com-
pels future rebirths. With this realization, Siddhartha
Gautama became the Awakened One.

For seven weeks the Buddha remained at the place
of his enlightenment, doubting whether others would
understand what he had learned. Yet moved by compassion, he determined to teach. He traveled to Varanasi
and in the Deer Park gave his first sermon on the Four
Noble Truths. These are discussed in Chapter 4. For the
next forty-five years, the Buddha traveled through northern India giving teachings and spiritual guidance to a
growing community of disciples. Since many men and
women wanted to take ordination from him, the Buddha
founded spiritual orders of monks and nuns—the
Sangha—giving them rules to observe to further their
spiritual development. The ordained disciples were
wandering mendicants. Lay disciples donated land to the

communities, so that monasteries could be established where monks and nuns could retreat during the rainy season. The Buddha and his followers lived simply, practicing the Buddha's teachings—the Dharma—and sharing it with others.

The Buddha's teachings profoundly influenced Indian society. He outlawed the prejudice and inequality of the caste system among his followers. Moreover, he acknowledged that women could attain liberation as well as men and allowed women to be ordained as nuns. By the time the Buddha died, or entered parinirvana, at the age of eighty, many kings had become his disciples, and his teachings had begun to spread beyond India into other countries.

The Buddha's Example

The life of the Buddha set a clear example that has relevance for our situation. Like us, Siddhartha was a human being who became aware of the basic problems of life and, driven by that awareness, made the shift from an orientation toward wealth, status, power, and pleasure toward a search for spiritual growth and self-evolvement. Though he lived in a culture seemingly quite different from our own, the Buddha passed through all the steps and stages which any person at any time must traverse in order to reach a higher state of inner development.

The first of these steps is a choice of lifestyles. Siddhartha grew up in a wealthy society, with a clear path toward a successful worldly career. Moreover, Siddhartha's father kept his son busy with luxuries and amusements to distract him from the universal problems of life and to entice him to follow in his father's footsteps.

Consume-oriented Western society provides most of us with the same conditions. All but the least fortunate members of society have the basic necessities of life, and

the majority of us have the opportunity to get the
education necessary to get well-paying jobs and to lead
comfortable lives. The constant bombardment of advertisements stimulates the desires that fuel the whole
economic and social system. The slick picture of happiness presented, for example, by many television
programs and movies keeps us from discovering the
hollowness which lies beneath the glittering surface.
Moreover, like Siddhartha's father, our society keeps old
people and sick people tucked away out of sight. Death
often takes place in hospitals and is seldom talked about.
Thus our society provides us with plenty of ways to
cover up and distract ourselves from thinking more
deeply about our situation. Caught up in society's deceptions, we often lose touch with reality and conveniently
forget that the good life cannot answer our existential
questions.

However, Siddhartha's society also provided him with
the model of an ascetic lifestyle and with teachers who
could offer him guidance on his spiritual search. We today also have access to the teachings of the world's
great spiritual traditions and the freedom and leisure to
practice them. Thus we, like Siddhartha, have the choice
of turning away from the pursuit of worldly gain toward
a life devoted to spiritual growth and to the benefit of
humankind.

A second parallel between the Buddha's life and our
own situation is the motivation for change. The three
rides that Siddhartha took with his charioteer, on which
he encountered old age, sickness, and death, shocked
Siddhartha into the realization of his own potential for
suffering and his own mortality.

In our world, too, a spiritual awakening can be cata-
lyzed by a close encounter with the sufferings of old
age, by a brush with serious illness, or by the death of a
friend or a family member. Moreover, old age, sickness,
and death can also be seen as representative of all the

problems, pains, and miseries we can encounter. Each of these conditions brings with it the threat of uncertainty. What will happen to me when I get old? How will *I* be able to cope with a life-threatening illness? What will happen to *me* when I die? Each of these questions carries within it the realization that we are born alone and will die alone and, in so doing, confronts us with the existential questions automatically linked with any human existence. Like Siddhartha, when we come face-to-face with questions regarding the purpose and meaning of life, our complacency is destroyed, and we are often driven to find the answers for ourselves. We, too, must determine what is of lasting value in the shadow of the threatening certainty of death, and what we can do to make our life truly meaningful.

As long as we are deceived by the illusions of a world of amusements and sensory pleasures and intoxicated by the empty promises of our consume-oriented society, we will seldom have the wish to look elsewhere. Only when we, like Siddhartha, are able to see the true nature of our situation and its real potential for misery will we be motivated to look for alternatives. This drive for finding a solution is represented by the mendicant that Siddhartha encountered on his fourth ride. The mendicant signifies the determination to seek the truth and indicates the direction in which to look—the spiritual dimension.

The third stage of the journey toward spiritual awakening is symbolized by Siddhartha's return to the palace, to his familiar environment. There Siddhartha was able to see through the deceptively attractive surface, and he determined to act on his realization immediately. Unfortunately, the same is not always true for us. Though we may sincerely wish to develop ourselves spiritually, the enticements of our familiar environment with its many pleasures often blunts our resolve. How often do we say, we will begin tomorrow to change our life, and then never do it. Or, if we finally begin, it may be too late to

accomplish much. Like Siddhartha, we must be firm in
the decision to seek spiritual growth and begin our
journey immediately, without procrastination.

Once we determine to take the radical step out of
consume-orientation and into the spiritual dimension, we
face, as did Siddhartha, the moment when we must
leave everything behind. Siddhartha's departure was
literal; he left kingdom, family, and status and went off
alone into the forest. Our renunciation can be more a
shift of mental attitude. As long as we are attached to
the things and experiences of this world, we are blocked
from a successful spiritual search. We need to reorder
our priorities and let go, not of the things themselves,
but of the inflated value we place on them—on the ever-
present striving to achieve more and more. Whether we
remain in our usual environment or not is beside the
point. Rather, we must see that material things are
incapable of bringing us lasting happiness.

If we, like Siddhartha, have really seen through the
deceit of consume-orientation, letting go of our materialistic strivings will be more a joyous release than a painful sacrifice. Our inner change of values and priorities as
we begin our spiritual journey can be as dramatic as
Siddhartha's outer transformation from a prince to a
homeless wanderer. When Siddhartha left his worldly
career behind, he did not know where to look for the
answers to his questions, nor whether the answers could
be found at all. But he was fully convinced that he had
been looking in the wrong direction. In abandoning his
former life, he was in effect setting out in the opposite
direction to see whether it held answers. To become a
wandering mendicant is to be a lone spiritual seeker
who, without material security, courageously faces
reality.

When we enter this stage of the spiritual journey, even
if we remain in our usual lifestyle and environment, we,
too, can feel like a mendicant: homeless, naked, alone,

insecure. Before beginning our spiritual search, we were often able to cover up these feelings, but now we are open and vulnerable. We have to acknowledge these fears in order to overcome them. It helps when we remember that the material security we have been building around us is itself impermanent and cannot really protect us from fears and suffering. When we accept the inherent uncertainty of life, we can also begin to experience the freedom we gain through letting go. As we get in touch with outward reality, we feel more inwardly authentic. The empty sensation we get when we fail to see a purpose to our existence starts to be filled, and life begins to acquire a deeper meaning.

The next stage of the spiritual journey is represented by the time Siddhartha spent studying various religious traditions and engaging in their practices. Yet when he realized that a particular method could not provide a permanent solution to his problems, he moved on. These actions demonstrate the importance of thorough investigation, analysis, learning, and study of whatever spiritual path we undertake, and willingless to search further.

The physical suffering and mental anguish Siddhartha experienced during his years of asceticism are similar to what a person on a spiritual search generally undergoes: hardships and diligent work to overcome obstacles. Like the Buddha during his meditation under the bodhi tree, we, too, will often be tempted by worldly influences which threaten to distract us from our purpose. We must remain firm, steady, and persistent in our endeavor if we are to defeat our negative habits of mind.

Achieving enlightenment, as the Buddha did, is not only the answer to our persistent existential dilemmas, but also the means of overcoming the individual sufferings of daily life. Enlightenment is a state beyond sorrow. By letting go of attachments and accepting things as they are, the Buddha transcended all pain and fear,

and achieved perfect balance and harmony with himself
and the universe. In his meditation, he gained deep
insight into the nature of all things, into the meaning
and purpose of existence, and into the interconnected-
ness of all life. With that wisdom, he achieved liberation
from the compulsion to remain within the cycle of
existence.

However, the Buddha also demonstrated clearly that
the spiritual journey is not ended with one's own
enlightenment. During the second half of his life, he
traveled tirelessly to help others, to spread his message,
and to form a strong spiritual community for the sake of
future beings. Even leaving the body through death does
not end or limit the vast capacity of an enlightened
being, like the Buddha. Through enlightened activity,
a Buddha continues to aid sentient beings in every
possible way until every being has achieved liberation
from suffering.

The Buddha's life story is an illustration and a challenge for every person who seeks the meaning and purpose of his or her individual life and of life within the
endless cycle of recurring existence. Many people in the
Buddha's time and in our own have followed his instructions, and many have actualized their fullest human
potential in attaining the highest level of spiritual
evolvement—Buddhahood.

3
Self-Liberation or Great Compassion

When the Buddha began to teach, there was no religion called Buddhism; there was only Buddha Shakyamuni as a spiritual teacher, his disciples, and other listeners of his words. How then did Buddhism develop from these simple beginnings into a world religion, with as many variations as exist today? The religious institutions that form the underpinnings of world Buddhism can be traced back to the first men and women who asked to be admitted to the group of disciples who traveled with the Buddha and helped spread his teachings. In time, when the number of disciples increased, Buddha gave his followers rules to support their mental training and to guide them in forming a spiritual community. These early ordained disciples were the first orders of Buddhist monks and nuns. It became traditional that during the rainy season, the Buddha and his disciples gathered in simple monasteries to do intensive meditation practice. The rest of the year they traveled to spread the Buddha's message.

After the death of the Buddha, his disciples came together to collect his discourses and advice and to verify their authenticity. Within three months of his death, five hundred monks gathered in a rainy season retreat to jointly confirm the teachings as recited by two of the

Buddha's chief disciples. At this first council, the process
of writing down the rules of the monastic orders—the
vinaya—and the discourses of the Buddha—the sutras
—was begun. A similar council was held one hundred
years later, attended by about seven hundred elder
monks from both northern and southern India. At
this council, delegates from the north and the south
disagreed about some particulars of the vinaya rules.
This disagreement led to the formation of two factions,
the southern Sthaviras and the northern Mahasanghikas.
Each group wrote down what it agreed were the rules in
their own language, the southern group in Magadha and
the northern group in Sanskrit. Because of the time and
distance involved, a third common council was not held.
After another one hundred years, the Sthaviras held a
council in their district, and soon after, the northern
Mahasanghikas met in Kashmir. From this split grew
the separate northern and southern Buddhist traditions.

Within these two groups, we must remember, much of
the tradition was transmitted orally. Students memorized
the teachings and stories and passed them on. Bit by bit,
the discourses of the Buddha and other texts related to
the tradition were collected and written down. The first
text to be standardized was the vinaya rules for monks
and nuns; the second was the sutras or discourses. Only
much later were the philosophical and metaphysical
aspects of Buddhism—the abhidharma—collected in text
form. These three groups of texts became known collec-
tively as the Tripitaka.

In the second half of the third century B.C.E., Buddhism spread to the island of Sri Lanka off the southern
tip of India. The monks of Sri Lanka canonized their
traditions of what the Buddha taught by translating the
Tripitaka into the Pali language during the first four
centuries C.E. The Tripitaka are the basic scriptures of
what came to be known as Theravadan or southern
Buddhism. Even today the Pali Canon is regarded by

Buddhists in Sri Lanka, Burma, Thailand, Cambodia, and Laos as the only true teachings of the Buddha. Any text which is not contained in that collection, either because it had spread only in the north or because it had not been written down at that time, is not recognized as an authentic teaching. In that sense, the Theravada comprises the conservative aspect of the Buddhist tradition.

In the first century B.C.E., the northern tradition of Buddhism separated further from the southern tradition along doctrinal lines. The northern tradition, which became known as the Mahayana, saw itself as metaphysically richer, as it included a number of discourses of the Buddha which had been hidden for a time and rediscovered. Unlike the Theravada, the Mahayana tradition accepted the new texts as valid teachings (most notably the Perfection of Wisdom Sutras) since they did not contradict the basic scriptures and since they contributed to one's inner development. The Mahayana also was able to adapt to the modern needs of the populace, and it encouraged more devotional activities. In that sense, the Mahayana makes up the progressive aspect of the Buddhist tradition. During the next several hundred years, the Mahayana flourished in India and spread into China, and from there, into Korea and Japan. The form of Mahayana Buddhism that developed in China and Japan became known as Ch'an or Zen Buddhism.

In the sixth century C.E., a third Buddhist tradition, the Tantrayana or Vajrayana, came to maturity. Philosophically, the Vajrayana is consistent with Mahayana Buddhism and can be considered its highest expression. The distictive feature of the Vajrayana is its inclusion of a number of secret oral traditions of ritual techniques and yoga practices—the tantras—which were transmitted privately from master to specially prepared disciple. A number of texts detailing these practices were written down during this period to prevent their loss. Because of its secrecy, the Vajrayana constitutes the esoteric and mystic part of the Buddhist tradition.

By the seventh century, Mahayana Buddhism, especially in its Vajrayana manifestation, began to be transmitted to the protected Himalayan region of Tibet. During the next several hundred years, many Indian masters were invited to teach in Tibet, and many Tibetans crossed the mountains to India to gather texts and teachings. The scriptures and oral commentaries collected in Tibet were translated into Tibetan by scholars at a system of great Buddhist monastic universities which developed in Tibet. Because of its remote location and its political and cultural isolation, Tibet became a storehouse of the texts and teachings of the greatest flourishing of Indian Mahayana Buddhism. Had Buddhism not become established outside of India, many of these traditions might have been lost when a Moslem invasion destroyed the great monastic centers of India around 1200 C.E.

This brief history of the development of the various Buddhist traditions illustrates an important truth. For any spiritual system to provide people of different cultures and different dispositions with a workable set of answers to their existential questions, that system must be able to change its form of practice, its institutional underpinnings, and even the language in which it is expressed, to meet new circumstances. Only if a religious system has this flexibility can it survive and continue as a living and viable tradition.

Over its twenty-five-hundred-year history, Buddhism has demonstrated this capacity for growth and change. Buddhism has transformed and has been transformed by every culture with which it has come in contact. It has adopted and integrated cultural and religious aspects of the places where it is practiced. However, the essential core of Buddhism has remained constant despite the different outward forms and methods through which that essence is expressed. Perhaps this is so because Buddhism has at its center a living experience—the Buddha's enlightenment under the bodhi tree, a non-conceptual experience that is in many ways beyond both comprehension and expression in words. The scholars of the great Buddhist universities in India and Tibet produced many metaphysical and philosophical treatises to express this experience, but, we should remember, any formulation of enlightenment in language is bound to be only an approximation. Buddhism has endured because it has never lost the uninterrupted stream of its connection to this living experience. Mahayana Buddhism in particular has never held dogmatically to an established doctrine and thus has never degenerated into a lifeless institution.

Mahayana Buddhism in the Tibetan tradition values its uninterrupted lineage of teachings and experiences which can be traced to the time of the historical Buddha. Many accomplished masters, up to the present day, have expressed their experiences within this living tradition in language and concepts suitable to the people of their time and culture. Outwardly, these various expressions may look different; in essence, they are the same.

In addition to its ability to adapt to time and culture, another factor which has contributed to the diversity of Buddhist thought is the Buddha's concern with the welfare of each living being. Different individuals have varying capacities for spiritual development; some have the ability to reach enlightenment in one lifetime, while others may think they can never reach it or may, in fact, need several lifetimes. In order to help every being make at least some progress toward enlightenment, Buddha and the later masters gave a variety of teachings to suit different capacities and dispositions. So that the faint-hearted would not be discouraged, they gave simplified theoretical explanations that were easy to understand and which outlined a goal that seemed easier to reach than fully enlightened Buddhahood. For those with greater capacity, they taught methods of attaining Buddhahood over the passage of many lifetimes. Finally, for those of the greatest capacity, they taught the quick but dangerous methods of the Vajrayana, through which Buddhahood can be reached within the span of one short human life.

A Divergence of Methods and Aims

The historical differences between the various Buddhist traditions are also reflected in a divergence of methods and aims. Buddhists in general hold to the view that compelled existence within the cycle of recurring rebirths—a cycle known as *samsara*—is characterized by suffering. The goal of the Theravadan practitioner is permanent extinction of one's personal suffering, which is the attainment of *nirvana*. A person who has achieved this state of self-liberation is called an Arhat. The Theravadan tradition teaches that Buddhahood is a very rare and difficult achievement, and therefore aims at the easier goal of becoming an Arhat, a being with limited capacities compared to a Buddha.

In order to attain Arhatship, one has to both free oneself from all desires and attachments to cyclic existence and its phenomena and realize selflessness —that is, the apprehension that persons and other phenomena lack inherent existence. To accomplish the first of these tasks, a practitioner must keep pure moral discipline, restrain himself or herself from worldly distractions and sense stimulations, and cultivate a firm sense of detachment. The basis of this detachment is the realization of impermanence, dissatisfaction, and selflessness.

The direct realization of selflessness is the second cause of attaining Arhatship. The mistaken view that persons and phenomena, including ourselves, exist

inherently—from their own side, not in dependence
on causes and conditions—is the root of our bondage
within cyclic existence. To cut this root and free oneself
from the cycle, one must cultivate meditative stability
and then, once the mind is quiet, carefully observe and
investigate the way persons and phenomena really exist,
until one perceives directly the emptiness of inherent
existence—the true nature of reality. Thus Theravadan
practice is characterized by the method of controlling
the body and mind through strict moral discipline and
meditative practice, and with self-liberation as the aim,
to detach completely from cyclic existence by means of
the realization of selflessness.

The Mahayana practitioner has both a wider choice of
methods and a more comprehensive aim. In addition to
his or her own suffering in samsara, the Mahayanist
recognizes the suffering of fellow beings and wishes
to help them. The sense of compassion awakened by
the recognition of others' suffering is cultivated and
expanded through meditations to train the mind until
the practitioner assumes complete dedication to and
responsibility for liberating every single living being
without exception from suffering. Thus one characteristic
method of Mahayana practice is the thought training
meditations to develop "great compassion."

To liberate all sentient beings from suffering, the
capacity of an Arhat is not sufficient. A Buddha's
omniscience is necessary to know how best to help
other beings. A Buddha also has the capacity to engage
in limitless activities, until every sentient being has
been liberated. Because a Mahayanist wants to be the
best help possible for other beings, he or she adopts as
a goal the state of ultimate personal development, which
is Buddhahood.

In order to achieve Buddhahood, the Mahayana offers
two distinct methods: a causal method, called the Perfection vehicle, and a result-oriented method, called the

Tantra vehicle. In the causal method, an aspirant practices the six types of perfect actions—perfect generosity, moral discipline, patience, enthusiastic effort, meditative concentration, and cultivation of wisdom—for a period of time designated traditionally as "three countless eons." In actual practice, a person works for the benefit of others over many, many lifetimes in order to build up a vast store of positive karmic imprints, or merit, which serve as the karmic cause for engaging in limitless Buddha activities. At the same time, the person meditates on emptiness unceasingly through many lives in order to achieve the wisdom mind of a Buddha. These two accomplishments are the eventual cause of Buddhahood.

Some Mahayana practitioners, however, find it unbearable to wait three countless eons to reach a level of power and ability from which they can effortlessly aid other suffering beings. Overwhelmed by their compassionate drive to help others, they seek a quicker method of achieving Buddhahood. The Tantra vehicle is such a path. It differs from the Perfection vehicle not in its final aim and attainments but in the method of progress and the speed of the progression. In addition to collecting the causes for Buddhahood by practicing the six types of perfect actions cultivated in the Perfection vehicle, the Tantric practitioner employs a result-oriented method from the outset. In meditation, the practitioner assumes the appearance, attitude, and activity of a Buddha, envisioned as a deity. This practice of deity yoga speeds up the accumulation of positive imprints. For the realization of emptiness, or wisdom, Tantra teaches special yogic practices to awaken the very subtle consciousness with which selflessness is most easily perceived. When a Tantric meditator combines the appearance of the deity with the simultaneous perception of noninherent existence, he or she achieves Buddhahood within this lifetime.

The form of Mahayana Buddhism practiced in Tibet encourages practitioners with the necessary foundation and motivation to enter the Tantric path. To build that foundation, one begins by taking stock of one's current situation and, realizing its suffering, develops the wish to gain liberation from the cycle of samsara. One also trains the mind in great compassion, the determination to achieve Buddhahood in order to liberate others from suffering. Propelled by that wish, one finally engages in Vajrayana practice to attain Buddhahood quickly, in this very life, for the welfare of all.

The Golden Wheel is the symbol of the religious law.

4
The Four Noble Truths

When the Buddha attained enlightenment, he experienced ultimate truth directly; that is, he saw and understood the true nature of phenomena and how phenomena are interconnected. In this enlightened state, the Buddha gained the wisdom of knowing whatever can be known. This wisdom is possible because an enlightened mind breaks through the limitations of the ordinary conceptual mind which is restricted to a relative perspective by its identification with the ego. Ego-identification leads the ordinary mind to conceive of the world as dualistic—as divided into self and other.

In his first discourse after achieving enlightenment, the Buddha arranged and expressed the deep insights he had gained into the nature of samsaric existence as the Four Noble Truths:

1) The truth of suffering.
2) The truth of the cause of suffering.
3) The truth of the cessation of suffering.
4) The truth of the path leading to cessation.

These four principles are accepted by virtually all Buddhists. They describe existence from the unique viewpoint of an enlightened being, one who sees reality

without the subjective distortions of an ego-centered
perspective.

The Truth of Suffering

The first Noble Truth, that life is characterized by
suffering or a sense of dissatisfaction, represents a deep
psychological and philosophical insight into existence.
According to this teaching, we fabricate our own model
of reality because of our ego-centered way of viewing the
world. We falsely see ourselves as separate from the rest
of the universe, a perception which engenders a feeling
of insufficiency and insecurity. In order to comfort and
protect ourselves from these feelings, we try to fill the
gaps. But to our dismay, we discover that we cannot get
everything our ego would like to have to make us feel
safe; moreover, we find that what we actually do have is
not able to protect us from threats to our existence. The
uncomfortable disjunction we experience causes us to
project our own wishful thinking out into the world,
and, in essence, make up our own ideal version of
reality.

Superficially, such magical thinking seems to help.
We project missing qualities and attributes onto external
things that match the images of our longings. Through
such projections, we keep up the hope that fulfillment
of our needs is still possible. All we need do is merely
come closer to the person, take part in the situation,
or possess the object of our desires. We also deny and
cover up uncomfortable aspects of the world, such as the
inevitability of death, to feel secure and protected.
Inadequacies in our own self-image are glossed over to
make us feel a little better about ourselves, and we deny
our emotional pains and fears. By projecting the pleasant
and denying the unwanted, we deceive ourselves with
an illusion. When our self-created dream world comes
into conflict with reality, as it inevitably must, our pains

and problems increase, and we sink deeper into a melodrama of our own creation.

The Buddha's message is that we have to stop running away. Avoidance can never solve a problem. Rather, we have to open up to the world as it is, see it, encounter it. Only when we stop denying and projecting and instead acknowledge the true situation can we realistically seek a solution. Even if the facts are painful and threatening, seeing them clearly is the beginning of finding an answer. The Buddha's first Noble Truth is an attempt to make us aware of the facts. He knew that until and unless we recognize that we are in trouble, we won't be motivated to look for a solution. From his enlightened viewpoint, he could see through our deceptions and our fabrications, through our pretending to be happy, although we are not. His first teaching makes us aware that we have been covering up dissatisfactions, denying problems, repressing pains and fears. It calls on us to arise from our deluded complacency and, by our own effort, follow the path he took and harvest the same fruit: lasting happiness and freedom from all sorrows.

In order to understand what such happiness implies, we need to examine in more detail the meanings of two important terms: *samsara* and *nirvana*. Samsara is not, as many people assume, a location or a place. It is, rather, an individual's experience of his or her existence. In psychological language, samsara is the melodrama in which a person is ensnared. We have already seen how our perceptions of the world are a subjective distortion of reality, based on the projections and denials of the ego. (Remember John and his son's subjective views of John's truck in Chapter 1.) The self-fabricated world, which is the accumulation of one person's deluded perceptions, is samsara. Thus samsara is more a mental state than a physical form of existence; it is the way an individual mind comprehends its existence. Moreover, samsara is, as we have said, the recurring cycle of lives that connects one to unsatisfactory existence. Because we distort reality, we become falsely attached to its pleasures. This attachment motivates us to act in ways that create the causes for us to be reborn again and again in lives that are similarly unsatisfactory.

The opposite condition to samsara is nirvana. It is the state of having transcended the misconceptions of ego-identity. To be in nirvana is to stop projecting fantasies and denying reality. Nirvana is a state beyond the deluded perceptions which create attachment to the phenomena of this world. A being in nirvana has passed beyond the sorrow of recurring rebirths in unsatisfactory lives into a state of harmony and bliss, free from dual-istic perceptions. Thus samsara and nirvana are not different environments or realms of existence. Samsara and nirvana exist side by side in our own world. We could sit at a table with two people, one of whom is caught up in samsara, a distorted view which incurs suffering, while the other abides in nirvana, an ability to see things as they are, which brings peace and harmony.

The first Noble Truth states that a being in samsara will not find lasting peace and happiness. Such a being will experience instead continuous dissatisfaction and suffering. The Buddha wanted to help us wake up from the nightmare of our samsaric melodrama. His statement demands a serious response. He tells us right from the start of the shortcomings and problems of samsaric existence in order to motivate us to gain the determina-tion to be free of it. By beginning his teaching with the uncomfortable idea that we ourselves and the world which we perceive are of a suffering nature, he chal-lenges us to examine and investigate our situation fairly.

When we take up the Buddha's challenge and begin to investigate, we soon find that there are many situations in life that cause us obvious physical pain, anxiety, and emotional distress. Everyone recognizes that illness, the loss of property, the death of loved ones, fear of failure, the loss of status or position, and the fear of death lead to suffering. These kinds of unhappiness are known as "the suffering of suffering"—all the events and experiences which one clearly recognizes as causes of pain.

The first Noble Truth, however, also encompasses a more subtle kind of suffering. When we analyze deeply, even those things we think make us happy turn out to be only moments of relief from a former pain. Say, for example, we are hiking up a steep mountain. Our muscles ache from the strain of the climb, and we are sweaty and out of breath. If only, we say to ourselves, we could reach the top and sit down. Finally, we reach our goal. Sitting down feels so good! Our new situation gives us a sensation of relief from the tension of climbing. Before long, however, the breeze which felt so refreshing at first begins to chill us, and we begin to think about dinner and worry about how long it will take to hike down. This new state of tension builds until we can no longer sit still and enjoy the view. Once again, we are restless and dissatisfied. To release the tension, we are driven once more to do something new. Of course whatever new thing we do is also incapable of bringing us lasting satisfaction; eventually, it, too, will change into discomfort. Our lack of recognition of this process keeps us constantly on the move, constantly searching for something new, something more, something better. This restlessness is characterisitic of "the suffering of change"—seemingly happy experiences that inevitably transform into pain.

Even if we were to free ourselves from the obvious sufferings of suffering and from the transformation of initially pleasant experiences into new kinds dissatisfaction, we have to contend with a third, most subtle kind of suffering. "All-pervading suffering" is the discomfort we feel when we remember that the future will definitely

bring us tremendous problems, even when we are not
experiencing any current difficulties. The knowledge,
or at least the apprehension, that any experience of
pleasure and satisfaction we may have will not last
subtly disturbs any sense of contentment we may have.
We sense that we are bound to experience future
suffering because everything that exists is subject to
constant change. This knowledge causes a pain which
pervades and underlies every samsaric experience.
Sometimes we are not aware of all-pervading suffering
since we are taken up by experiencing the stronger,
more overt varieties.

The first Noble Truth asks us to examine our current
situation carefully to see whether it is as the Buddha
describes. Only when we realize for ourselves the truth
of the Buddha's vision will we generate the urge to do
something to change the situation.

The Cause of Suffering and Its Cessation

The Buddha realized, further, that everything that exists
in the world depends on some cause or condition. Since
suffering exists, it must have a cause. In the second
Noble Truth, the Buddha taught that the cause of all
types of samsaric suffering is delusions and karma.
Karma is a Sankrit word that means "action." Karma
includes all our mental and physical actions and their
inevitable consequences. The idea of karma is discussed
more fully in Chapter 6. We can define *delusions* as the
disturbed mental states which motivate us to act and
react in ways that create consequences.

We have already identified one important kind of
delusion as the distorted views associated with identifying ourselves with the ego. But what is the cause of our
characteristic identification with the ego? According to
the Buddha, the root cause of suffering is a basic
delusion called ignorance. *Ignorance* means both "not

knowing'' and ''wrong knowing.'' Because we have the innate feeling of existing as an independent self, we wrongly assume that we are separate from the outside world, which appears as existing independent of causes and conditions. This false set of perceptions leads us to make dualistic discriminations: I like this; I do not like that. This experience will be good for me; this experience will be bad. Such dualistic discriminations lead to our developing attachment for those things and experiences that make us feel good, or enhance the ego, and aversion for those things and experiences that make us feel bad, or threaten the ego. In turn, attachment and aversion motivate us to engage in all types of activities. Out of attachment, we covet and cling, defend possessions and property, even steal. Out of aversion, we experience anger and hatred, hurt people physically and emotionally, start wars, even murder. Thus all the pains and miseries of the world we inhabit arise from delusions, which stem ultimately from ignorance.

The Buddha's third Noble Truth points to the way out of this trap. Of the two causes of suffering mentioned in the second Noble Truth—delusions and karma—delusions are more important, because they come first in time. Without the delusions of attachment and aversion, and their root cause, the delusion of ignorance, we would not be motivated to act in such ways to create the karmic causes of rebirth in samsara. Moreover, eliminating delusions also prevents negative actions which we have committed in the past from ripening into the consequence of a samsaric future. It is, in fact, the endless cycle of delusions—ignorance, attachment, and aversion —and their consequences which connect us to samsara.

The mechanism of samsara is like a machine: one cog drives a wheel, which turns another, which keeps the whole machine in motion. Ignorance leads to deluded states of mind such as attachment and aversion. When these delusions arise in our mind, they make us unhappy and motivate us to act in ways that build the karmic causes to keep our melodrama going. Since samsaric existence is a result, if we eliminate its causes —delusions and their consequences—the result can never arise. Thus if we want to escape from the endless cycle of samsaric rebirths, our point of attack must be the delusions.

The Path

Over the centuries, Buddhist masters have taught many techniques for attacking delusions. Some of these methods are introduced in Part II. Before we begin on them, however, we must be convinced that their basis is sound.

Is it really possible, we might ask, to eliminate our delusions once and for all? What must we do to accomplish this goal? The answer to this question is embodied in the Buddha's fourth Noble Truth. This teaching describes a series of practical actions and attitudes— a path—through which we can stop our suffering and attain nirvana. This path has three main sections, called by later masters the "three higher trainings": ethics, concentration, and wisdom.

The three higher trainings represent the practical part of Buddhism. They outline for us what we must actually do to follow a spiritual path. The three higher trainings are also interrelated. In order to eliminate ignorance, we must realize the true nature of the self. This realization is the principle goal of the higher training of wisdom. Through analysis, investigation, and observation, it is possible to realize that the self and phenomena do not exist the way we perceive them. Yet their mode of existence is very subtle, and with our normal distracted mind, our analysis would not be very successful. Therefore, it is necessary to calm the mind and to develop the ability to concentrate single-pointedly on whatever subject we choose as a focus. This ability is developed through the higher training of concentration. Our normal way of living, however, fueled as it is by desires and other emotions, gives us little time or motivation to practice concentration. This is where the higher training in ethics comes in. Training in ethics teaches us to overcome gross external and internal distractions so that we can get started on the spiritual path.

With this overview of their interconnections in mind, let us look at each training in more detail. The higher training in ethics is designed to give us more time, rest, and space. The fundamental shift from consume-orientation toward spirituality is the very first step in this training. Only when we have realized the futility of seeking happiness through external means and made spiritual development a priority will we stop wasting time accumulating material wealth, striving for status, or indulging in short-lived sense pleasures. Once this basic shift has been accomplished, we keep our resolve by maintaining ethical discipline.

When we think about the higher training of ethics, it is also important to note at the outset that Buddhist ethics are based on practical or pragmatic considerations, not on judgments of what actions are good and what actions are evil. Actions are called "negative" if they bring us or others unhappiness and thus hinder our spiritual development; "positive" actions, on the other hand, create happiness for ourselves and others and bring us closer to liberation or nirvana. In general, Buddha advised us to avoid ten actions that contribute to our suffering and the suffering of others: killing, stealing, sexual misconduct, lying, slander, harsh speech, gossip, coveting others' possessions, malicious actions, and wrong views. If we consider these actions and their consequences carefully, it is easy to see that they are what underlie the samsaric melodrama.

Simultaneously to observing ethics, the Buddha

advised us to practice introspection and mindfulness—
aspects of the second higher training in concentration
—so that we begin to get aware of what is happening
around us. We start to see who we are, how we act, and
what the results of these actions are in our lives and the
lives of others. We try to identify the habitual patterns
that bring us freedom and harmony and develop ways to
support and further these patterns. At the same time,
we try to pinpoint the actions that create problems and
conflicts and work to change and eliminate these actions.
Through mindfulness we begin to see what encourages
and what blocks our inner development. Supported by
some personal discipline and through the application of
meditative techniques, we can target specific negative
habitual patterns, reduce unwanted habits, and familiarize ourselves with positive ways of viewing ourselves
and the world.

The second higher training, concentration, also helps
us gain *shamatha*, or "tranquil abiding"—the ability to
concentrate effortlessly on any object or subject we wish
to focus on. Beginning with short meditations focusing
on a fixed object and progressively prolonging them, we
learn to let go of subtle distractions and prepare ourselves to engage in the meditations of the higher training
of wisdom.

The third higher training provides meditative techniques aimed at developing the realization of ultimate
reality. Being well prepared with a clear and still
mind and a steady focus, we can come to see that
nothing, no being and no thing, exists in and of itself.
In other words, all created things depend on causes or
conditions. This is not to say that the things we see and
experience do not exist. They most certainly do, but only
in a relative sense, not absolutely. In order to realize the
true mode of existence, one first establishes an intellectual understanding of emptiness by means of logical
reasoning and analysis; then through repeated medita-

tive observations, one works up to a direct perception of that truth.

A unique quality of Buddhahood is the ability to perceive relative reality—the world as it appears to us normally—and absolute reality—the truth that persons and phenomena lack independent self-existence—simultaneously. When we train in the higher training of wisdom, our goal is to work toward attaining this level of perception. When we have done so, we, too, attain Buddhahood.

5
Meditation: The Practical Method of Inner Development

An athlete who wants to build up body control, flexibility, and strength has to engage in physical exercises and fitness training. If instead of exercising, a tennis player, for example, watches matches on television and reads accounts of tournaments in the sports pages of magazines and newspapers, the player might become a knowledgeable tennis insider, well-versed in the rules and terminology of the game. But the player's body would still be stiff and weak, and his or her tennis game would not improve at all.

Theoretical information and knowledge can be useful, but it can never substitute for practical exercise. Theory aids a practice, and it is sometimes necessary to know the theory behind a practical exercise before trying it. But even the greatest theory can never bring results if it is not put into action. Therefore, practice is absolutely necessary for any development to take place, whereas theory is only an aid. As this rule applies to the athlete, so too it applies to the spiritual seeker. Thus a person looking for self-evolvement, for more peace and inner harmony, must engage in spiritual exercise.

A big problem in our brain-dominated culture is that we often confuse intellectual knowledge with authentic inner development. In many Eastern cultures, children learn very early the practical skills needed to make a living or to supply a family's needs. In the educational system in the West, however, children are fed for ten years with information and accumulate knowledge rather than practical skills. No wonder we think that knowledge is all that is necessary for spiritual development. We receive admiration, praise, and rewards if we are well-educated. In many modern professions, all that is required is a rational, working brain. If any practical work needs to be done, like hanging a picture in our office, we call the maintenance department to send up a manual worker to hammer the nail into the wall.

We have to realize that spiritual development is an art, a practical skill, a way of behaving and acting, a transformation of our whole being—it is becoming an authentic person. Information and knowledge are just abstract ideas and items in brain storage. But love, compassion, strength, and wisdom are inner qualities which, having been cultivated within the individual, become actual parts of the person. The idea and theory of love is just a mental concept, but love itself as an integrated quality of a person is a manifest state of being, a behavior which becomes obvious in activities, of which the individual himself or herself becomes the expression.

Storing information in our brain is one thing, but integrating the meaning of the information is another. Information is a medium to convey a message, but only the manifestation and materialization of the message is a real thing. Spiritual development should be a real thing. It must be the actualization of a theory, not just the theory itself.

It is very important that we see clearly what real inner development is and that we do not mix it up with intellectual knowledge. We should understand that theoretical knowledge can support a spiritual practice, but only the practice itself can be an actual cause of spiritual

attainment. All that can be said for theory is that it is
a condition contributing to spiritual development, but
one that is sometimes not essential to the result.

Given this, we now come to the questions: What kind
of spiritual practice should we do to integrate new
spiritual values into our lives? How can we transform
abstract or intellectual ideas about spirituality into a
concrete way of living? In most spiritual traditions the
answer is simply meditation. What do we mean by that?

In brief, we can say that meditation is a kind of
practical training needed to gain actual inner development. It is a method through which we can change or
eliminate unwanted habits, cultivate and integrate
beneficial qualities, and gain wisdom. Because it serves
various purposes, meditation is not just one single
exercise. Rather it is a series of specific techniques
targeted for the different stages of spiritual development.

An athlete, to return to our earlier example, must
engage in many different exercises. A tennis player
might begin with a basic program of weight training and
conditioning, and later shift to more difficult exercises
aimed toward developing the serve, court coverage, or
shot placement. Every part of the game will have its
own particular exercises. Some exercises may build on
the development gained from an earlier stage of training.
Such a systematic exercise program will allow the player
to achieve the highest level of skill in the shortest
amount of time.

The same methodology applies to spiritual training.
A variety of meditations prepare the practitioner and
boost his or her level of development up to the ultimate
achievement of Buddhahood.

The Purpose of Buddhist Meditation

We now turn to an overview of the various Buddhist
meditation techniques and explore their purposes and

functions. Later chapters give specific instructions for practicing these meditations. Through examining them here in general, we will get a picture of the whole practical path of Buddhism.

The usual problem at the beginning of spiritual training is our restless mind, which is overloaded by sensory stimulation, mental impressions, information, emotional states, and so forth. Our daily obligations create stress and pressure, and we are pulled and pushed by our desires and aversions. The result is that we are often restless and nervous. It is impossible to gain any real spiritual development while our mind is so occupied that it jumps up and down like a crazy monkey. Thus we need first of all to calm down, to get settled and relaxed.

The meditation technique targeted for this stage is just sitting in a quiet place and observing our breath as it naturally flows in and out. If we practice this meditation, in a short time our mind will be clearer, and we will feel better. If we practice this meditation regularly, our whole life will become more peaceful, our level of stress and tension will be reduced, and our mental state will become more balanced.

Once we are acquainted with observing the breath, we can let go of the breath as an object of focus, and practice just remaining in the here and now. By letting go of everything and abiding in the present, we create a kind of mental space. This sense of space has a healing influence on our overactive mind and on our whole being.

The next step in meditation is a solid training in awareness. If we want to work on our personality to change unwanted patterns, we first have to get to know them. Likewise, if we want to gain insight and wisdom about ourselves and the world, we first have to see the world and ourselves as they are. Thus conscious recognition is a basic prerequisite for inner development.

The meditations that can make us aware of ourselves and of the circumstances that surround us are called mindfulness training. This training consists of four major steps: First we learn to observe our own body, physical sensations, and our sense perceptions of sights, sounds, smells, and tastes. Second, we watch our feelings of attraction or liking, aversion or disliking, and neutrality toward the things we encounter. Third, we observe our mental and emotional states. Finally, we become mindful of our thoughts themselves and of their content. These four categories include all possible perceptions and mental faculties.

After we gain familiarity with each of these four objects of awareness, we will be able to recognize what is going on inside our minds and outside in the world around us. As we continue our mindfulness meditation, we will begin to see how the various external conditions and objects of perception relate to each other and how we function in and relate to the outside world. Through these observations, we gain deeper insight into the nature of existence. We also start to see who we are, what we do and why, and what results our various actions bring about. In this way, we learn to distinguish between beneficial behavior and behavior that causes us conflicts and problems.

At this point, we can start to change our personality actively by means of the next type of meditative practice—analytical meditation. Unlike mindfulness meditation, the purpose of which is to sharpen our awareness of what is happening inside and outside ourselves, analytical meditation helps us to break unwanted habitual patterns, cultivate appropriate behavior, and integrate inner values and insights.

Mindfulness meditation can bring similar results, but it works more slowly. Passively observing and watching what is going on as one does in mindfulness practice can lead to insights and realizations, and thus influence our habitual patterns. Analytical meditations, however, bring results more immediately.

In analytical meditation, we thoroughly investigate a mental attitude, inner value, quality, or habitual pattern. As we do, we come to the conclusion that our attitudes, values, qualities, and patterns have not always been part of us. Rather they have been conditioned. This means that at some time in the past, we got accustomed to, learned, or adopted each of them. As we investigate further, we find that sometimes we became familiar with a particular way of thinking or acting through repeated contact. Then the behavior or attitude became a habit, and finally a part of our personality. Other times, we find that a single striking experience caused a permanent change in our attitude or behavior. In either case, we find that each of our thoughts and actions depends on certain conditions. Thus what we are right now has been conditioned by previous events and experiences that formed and shaped our personality.

Perhaps our investigation will show that a particular imprint on our consciousness was made by our parents, teachers, or by society at large, often without any control from us and sometimes even against our wishes. We may not even be aware of some of our habits and their consequences. Through analytical meditation we can check up and decondition ourselves, throw out what we do not want, and consciously choose alternative ways of thinking and acting. How do we do this?

The first step is acknowledging that our present personality has been formed through past conditions and influences. Since this is so, we can now deliberately set up new conditions that can act to change our former habits. This is why mindfulness meditation is a necessary preliminary. Mindfulness practice provides a basis of self-awareness, so that we can identify the external events that cause the particular problem behavior we are trying to change.

Once we have discerned the problem and its causes, we examine the consequences of our habitual way of thinking or acting to determine if the pattern is a good one or if it has been leading to conflicts or problems. If we find that the behavior or attitude leads to problems, we analyze carefully many situations in which this has occurred in order to convince ourselves of the dis-advantages of this way of thinking or acting. Thus through analytical thinking, we gain a deeper under-standing of the behavior or attitude and develop and strengthen the wish to alter it.

Through repeated analysis and contemplation, the intention to stop a particular habit of mind or behavior gets stronger and stronger. With this basis of support, we can begin to work on actual changes. Say, for example, we are trying to lessen our anger. By remem-bering countless examples of angry behavior and its consequences, we train ourselves in formal meditation sessions to integrate our understanding of the destruc-tiveness of anger and imagine alternative ways of acting. Then we work to put our new understanding and intention into practice. Supported by our practice of mindfulness, we catch ourselves more and more often in actual situations in which anger arises. Using the reasons and intentions we have built up during our analytical meditations, we remind ourselves again and again to act differently, and we apply the antidotes to anger we have cultivated during our formal meditation sessions.

As we gain familiarity with the new behavior, it comes more and more easily, until the new behavior itself becomes a positive pattern. Using this methodology, we can break our negative habits and cultivate positive ones. Thus analytical meditations can actually change our personality.

To review, we can say that the meditation of creating space helps us to be more relaxed and clears our over-loaded mind. Mindfulness meditation trains us to be aware of the present moment, while analytical medita-tions actively change our habitual patterns. The final steps in this sequence are training in concentration and, finally, formal meditation on selflessness.

On the Buddhist path, most of the earlier meditations are actually preparations for the meditation on selflessness. Changing our habitual patterns will definitely bring us more space, contentment, and freedom. Such changes stop many of our conflicts and bring us a deeper understanding of ourselves and the world as many of our delusions and wrong views are cleared away. However, insights such as these will do nothing to alter our deep-rooted belief in the inherent existence of ourselves and the objects we perceive in the world around us. No matter how many habitual patterns we change, we will still perceive everything as having a real, permanent, independent existence from its own side. This wrong view is the actual root of all our problems and thus has to be eliminated. For this, we need the meditation on selflessness.

In order to succeed with the profound meditation on selflessness, however, we need to develop the single-pointed concentration that allows us to stay focused on an object of contemplation for as long as we like. To develop this ability, we have to learn concentrated meditation. For example, we may start with short sessions in which we concentrate on a visualization of a Buddha image. By learning to focus the mind unwaveringly on an intended object, we train ourselves to stay with it for longer and longer periods of time. As our concentration develops, we make our sessions longer and longer, until we have developed sufficient concentration to meditate on selflessness.

The actual meditation on selflessness begins with an analysis of how the self appears to us. Next we investigate whether such a self can be found within the person or outside. The point here is that if a self exists, it has to be found either within the person or outside—there is no third possibility. By such investigation, we will find that no matter how hard we try, we cannot find such a self. We must conclude, therefore, that the self does not exist at all as we perceive it. Through repeated analysis, we eventually gain a direct perception of selflessness.

Since our wrong view of self is such a deep-rooted habit, we will still have the tendency to fall back into our old perceptions. Because of this tendency, we must engage in longer periods of meditation on selflessness with the goal of eliminating all our remaining subtle incorrect mental attitudes, together with their imprints on our consciousness. This meditation, combined with the complete accumulation of the positive potential to accomplish the aim of enlightenment, leads one to the stage of no-more-learning, which is the attainment of ultimate perfection or Buddhahood.

6
Karma

Modern physics has taught us that energy and matter do not disappear, nor do they arise out of nothingness. Rather, matter and energy engage in a constant dance of change and interaction, the rhythm of which depends on causes and conditions. On a material level, every result has a cause, and every result becomes, in turn, a cause bringing new consequences. Sometimes the results are not apparent to our senses, as in the case of events occuring at the molecular level. However, the sophisticated measuring instruments used by physicists provide ample evidence of the universality of cause and effect at all levels of existence.

Eastern philosophy has long known about the law of cause and effect. For thousands of years Eastern masters have taught that the same principle that modern science has demonstrated in the physical world applies as well to the mental and spiritual planes of existence. The great spiritual masters of the East, like Buddha Shakyamuni, achieved direct insight into the law of cause and effect. According to their experience, this law is more subtle and more far-reaching than the causes and effects we can perceive with our ordinary awareness. The Buddha taught that the law of cause and effect applies not only to the material world, but to mental functioning as well.

This law explains the connection between mind and
matter as a mutual interaction. In other words, physical
actions influence our mental states, and mental impulses
influence our physical environment.

Another name for the universal law of cause and effect
is the *law of karma*. As explained earlier, *karma*, which
means "action," refers to all the actions of our body,
speech, and mind that follow from a mental intention.
According to the Buddha, every action leaves an imprint,
or potential, upon our mindstream. When these imprints
meet with proper conditions, they serve as causes to
bring about corresponding results. In general, positive
actions are the causes of positive or pleasant results, and
negative actions are the causes of negative or unpleasant
ones.

It is important to remember that neither the Buddha
nor the other Eastern spiritual masters who taught about
karma created the law, any more than Sir Isaac Newton
created the law of gravity. They simply had the insight
to describe the system of cause and effect that is part of
the natural functioning of the universe. Moreover, the
karmic law is not a systems of rewards and punish-
ments, through which the Buddha or any other authority
causes people to suffer for their wrongdoings. Rather,
any unpleasant results we experience have been
determined by our own actions.

Four Karmic Principles

The Buddha described in detail the functioning of the
karmic law in his teachings. In particular, he taught four
principles that explain how the law of cause and effect
works in the lives of beings. The first of these is that
karma is definite. In other words, every action of body,
speech, and mind creates the potential to bring about
a result similar to the cause. Positive actions bring only
pleasant results (and not any other kind), while negative

actions bring only unpleasant results. If we plant a tulip bulb, only a tulip will grow, and not an onion.

The second karmic principle is that *karma is fast growing*. This means that small causes can bring large results. Just as a snowball rolling down a mountain can eventually cause an avalanche, so too a seemingly insignificant action can lead to serious consequences. This principle is important because we often rationalize our negative behavior—for example, calling our untruths "white lies." The second principle of karma reminds us that all actions—even so-called "white lies"—have consequences. Similarly, every small thing we do to help another being can be the cause of significant positive results for us in the future.

The third karmic principle states that *if the cause has not been created, the result will not be experienced*. Perhaps this feature of the karmic law can best be explained by an example. Say that a plane crashes. Some people are killed, though others, perhaps even ones sitting nearby, walk away unhurt. How can this be explained? Quite simply, in some lifetime, each person who died created the cause for this kind of death; the others on the plane did not. Thus according to karmic law, the operation of the universe is invariably just. Only if someone has personally created the cause can he or she experience the corresponding result. Without the cause being created, there will be no result, now or in the future.

The fourth karmic principle is that *the results of actions will definitely be experienced*. Every completed action—even an action that was committed a long time ago, or one which no one knows about—creates an imprint on our mindstream. This imprint does not lose its potential until the right conditions cause it to ripen or it is eliminated or reduced by opposing forces, such as purification meditations. Karma is not, however, a kind of predestination. Many factors can mitigate or even prevent a karmic imprint from ripening. For example, living an

ethical life and engaging in meditative practices to purify
a negative imprint can prevent it from bringing an
undesirable result. Conversely, anger can keep a positive
karmic imprint from ripening into a beneficial result.
Thus there is enough room for us to do and undo.

The essential message of these four principles is that
each living being is the architect of its future. If we are
the ones who act in a certain way, we are the ones who
will experience the results. No one can give us their
positive or negative karmic imprints, and no one can
take ours away. Thus happiness does not depend on the
grace of a higher being, nor is anyone else to blame for
one's own misfortunes. By our actions in the present,
we create our own future.

Gaining Confidence in the Karmic Law

Unless we are confident that the karmic law as described
by the Buddha is an accurate picture of the way the universe functions, karma will be just another interesting
theory. Though our knowledge of karma is based on the
observations of great spiritual masters, few of us would
be willing to change our behavior simply on their advice.

How do we, in fact, decide what to believe? In everyday matters, we seldom subject ideas to rigorous tests.
Usually we believe what we read in the newspaper or
hear on television, trusting the authorities and the
opinions of the majority to tell us what is true. Sometimes we make decisions or even build our lives on ideas
we ourselves have not proven to be true. Living in such
a glut of information and theory, it is impossible for us
to examine critically every new idea we encounter. Moreover, even if we want to verify a piece of information for
ourselves, often we cannot. For example, if a medical
journal reports that tomatoes grown in a particular state
have been sprayed with a chemical believed to cause
cancer, we immediately stop buying that state's toma-

toes. We do not test the tomatoes ourselves to see
if they are tainted with the chemical, nor do we conduct
research into the connection between the chemical and
cancer. Instead, we rely on the authorities, as it is
impossible to personally check all information.

In cases where expert opinions vary, we have learned
to use our critical faculties to choose which authority to
believe. If the Tomato Growers' Association, to continue
the example, argues that the chemical in question is
harmless and only makes the color of the tomatoes more
appealing, we would probably question their motivation,
remain suspicious, and continue to avoid tomatoes. In
other words, we use our logical mind to select which
source to trust.

When we hear about a new theory in science, we
probably employ a combination of these methods. First,
we try to comprehend the theory intellectually. Perhaps
we seek answers by reading articles or books. After
evaluating the idea using logic, common sense, and
previous experience, we examine the credentials of the
authority making the new claim. If the theory passes
these tests, we are inclined to believe it.

This model is perhaps the most useful when we
undertake proving the truth of an idea like karma. The
Buddha warned us clearly in many discourses not to
accept any of his ideas on faith alone. Do not believe
what the books or the tradition teaches you, he once
said. Do not believe what the elders or your parents say.
Rather, check, examine, and investigate all of my
teachings. Accept what you find to be true for yourself
and live accordingly. Thus we must proceed carefully
when we are confronted with an idea like karma. The
law of karma, like the question of reincarnation which is
discussed in Chapter 7, is such a fundamental question,
with such far-reaching implications for our lives, that we
should heed the Buddha's advice and consider carefully
whether to believe it.

How could we use the previously outlined model to investigate the idea of karma? The first step is to gain an intellectual understanding of karma. This chapter presented an overview of the Buddha's teachings on karma. Many of the books on the Recommended Reading list contain more detailed information on the topic. Reading and thinking about this material may be a good place to begin.

Next, we might use logic, common sense, and previous experience to investigate karma. In daily life it is fairly easy to observe the obvious operation of causes and effects. For instance, a friendly smile and a cheery "good morning" are more likely to win us the good opinion of our coworkers than a scowl and a grunt. Similarly, a person who habitually tells lies will lose his or her credibility and may be more likely to be lied to by others. Though there may be exceptions, as a general rule, we can say that in observable human interactions, we reap what we sow.

On a subtle level, it is more difficult to observe the functioning of the karmic law. Some people seem to be very lucky and effortlessly get what they need; others meet with one setback or obstacle after another. Are these differences purely accidental or does a subtle causal relationship underlie them?

At this point we might ask why we should consider the Buddha or any other Eastern spiritual master who has described the workings of karma to be a proper authority. One can answer this question by recalling the events of the Buddha's life story and by thinking about the specifics of his teachings. Both the Buddha's biography and his message demonstrate that he was completely dedicated to the welfare of other beings. Futhermore, we can see that everything he said or did was motivated by compassion for others. Since this is so, it is illogical to think that he would deceive us. We can also examine his other precepts, such as the truth of suffering or the value of meditation. Since we can easily see the truth of these ideas, perhaps we can give the idea of karma the benefit of the doubt. Many things exist which we are not able to perceive directly, such as radio waves and bacteria. If a trustworthy person like the Buddha, who has given us so much other useful and proven advice, says that karma exists, and since nothing logically contradicts his words, we may wish to rely on his authority.

One way to answer this question is to think about what we have experienced or observed about psychological functioning. We can all think of cases in which a traumatic experience, perhaps even one which has been completely forgotten or repressed, influences a person's current behavior. For example, say that a young man experiences a trauma when his girlfriend breaks up with him. This event plants the idea in his unconscious that he is not worthy of being loved. As time passes, though he is not conscious of the pattern, the young man experiences relationship after relationship with women who eventually break up with him. According to his conscious mind, of course, this result is the last thing he wants, but the events of his past cause him to manipulate circumstances to encounter the loss of love and to experience his own unworthiness again and again. In the same way that subtle subconscious imprints manipulate the way we act in the present, imprints from actions we have committed in the past—even in previous lifetimes—shape what happens to us right now. Both subconscious psychological imprints and the karmic imprints on our subtle consciousness are generally unavailable to our conscious mind. Under hypnosis or in deep meditative states, however, memories may arise reaching back into childhood and even into former lives.

Thus it may not be too difficult for us to accept the idea that our subtle levels of consciousness contains imprints of whatever we did or encountered in the past.

Whether we like them or not makes no difference; imprints from the past automatically push through and move us into certain situations. Accepting this idea may help us explain many things that seem on the surface arbitrary or unfair. When we see a kind person die young or a cruel person acquire wealth and power, for example, we might doubt whether karma is operating. If we think back to our intellectual understanding of karma, though, we might remember that the consequences of karma often stretch over several lifetimes. Perhaps, we may then reason, the person who was kind in this life was a hunter who killed many animals in a previous life, while the cruel but wealthy person was a generous benefactor in a previous existence. The teachings on karma state further that only an enlightened being like the Buddha has the vision to see exactly what specific combination of actions led to a particular result.

This brings us to the third level of our investigation—the question of authority. We have seen that it is possible to observe the cause-and-effect relationship in many of our actions and experiences. However, the more distant the causes, such as those from previous lifetimes, the more difficult for us to perceive their connection to effects. We must conclude, therefore, that it is beyond our capacity to prove conclusively that the karmic law exists. We can and should investigate the question as thoroughly as we can, but in the end, we have to rely on a proper authority.

The Two Golden Fish symbolize the beings saved from the ocean of earthly life and suffering.

7
Reincarnation

Rebirth is part of the prevailing worldview in many Eastern countries. For this reason, many people in the East never question whether or not they "believe" in reincarnation. In the West, on the other hand, the Judeo-Christian concept of reward or punishment in the after-life or the equally powerful belief in the materialism of modern science constitute worldviews in which rebirth has no natural place.

Given this, when we in the West look at theories like reincarnation, we should try to keep our cultural conditioning in mind. We have been brought up since childhood with a set of beliefs that opposes the continuation of consciousness from life to life. In order to consider objectively other theories about what happens to consciousness after death, we have to set aside our familiar view and try to consider the question with a mind free of preconceptions.

When we let go of our habitual biases, many after-death theories present themselves. Perhaps death means the total annihilation of consciousness. Perhaps, as Christianity teaches, good people reside eternally in heaven, while sinners suffer eternal damnation. Or, perhaps, consciousness—like other forms of energy—

simply changes form and leaves the old body to connect to a new one.

To examine these various possibilities, we might employ a methodology similar to the one we used in considering karma. We can begin by reading and thinking about the investigations and other evidence that support various after-death theories. In the light of this information, we can think about our own experiences and see whether a belief in reincarnation helps answer questions that puzzled us previously. Finally, we can consult authorities and see what the great teachers of the past have said about the subject. Based on these investigations, we may be able to form our own opinion and choose a belief system that makes the most sense to us.

Evidence for Reincarnation

In the last thirty years, Western researchers have begun to collect evidence about reincarnation. Some have concentrated on people who demonstrate "spontaneous recall"—recollections by a child or adult of an immediately preceding life. Others have focused on "hypnotic regression"—recalling details of a previous life under hypnosis. Most contemporary studies have applied the methodology of Western science. After the evidence is collected, much care is taken to verify the details given by informants. Many possible explanations are considered before the assumption is made that the evidence indicates a past life.

A famous recent study of spontaneous recall was done by Dr. Ian Stevenson, a professor of psychiatry at the University of Virginia. Stevenson recorded memories by children and some adults that were suggestive of past lives, interviewed family members and neighbors, and investigated whenever possible the site of the recalled life, talking to people who might have known the person who died. Stevenson also rigorously investigated other possible explanations for the memories, such as genetic memory, telepathy, spirit communication, possession, and fraud. The results of Stevenson's work were published in *Twenty Studies Suggestive of Reincarnation* (1974, 1978) and other books.

One of the possibilities Stevenson considered to explain his evidence was *cryptomnesia*. This term refers to the process of learning things in the usual way and then forgetting the source of the learning. When the previously acquired information pops up in current thinking, it appears to come from a hidden or mysterious source. Perhaps, Stevenson hypothesized, a person recalling a "memory" from a past life is in fact remembering something he or she read, saw a picture of, or heard someone talking about. Cryptomnesia does happen in everyday life, such as when a composer writing a song unconsciously includes a melody from another composer's work that he or she heard once but has since forgotten. Stevenson's study, however, contains many cases in which subjects recalled information that they could not have acquired in a normal way, such as the ability to speak a foreign language or details about life in a foreign country not known to anyone who has had contact with the subject. British researcher Francis Story reports that one young subject was able to perform Indian dances, which seems to corroborate the subject's claim to having been a dancer in India in a previous life (*Rebirth as Doctrine and Experience*, 1975).

Another explanation for the evidence collected by researchers is telepathy. Perhaps the person recalling a past life is really "reading the mind" of a living person who has knowledge of the details being recalled. However, this explanation does not hold up either. Some of Stevenson's subjects reported details that no one but the deceased person could have known, such as unpaid debts, unknown to surviving relatives but confirmed by investigators, or the secret circumstances of the person's

death. Even in cases in which the information recalled is
known to others, it is significant that subjects recalled
only information relating to a particular person and that
subjects felt a strong identification with the deceased
person. Other people with telepathic powers do not
think that they *are* the person whose thoughts they are
reporting.

Stevenson also considered and rejected several other
possible explanations for the data he collected. Fraud can
be excluded since, in many cases, it would have required
a complicated conspiracy between informants, none of
whom had a motive for such collusion. Genetic memory,
an inborn imprint similar to the instincts of animals, can
also be ruled out, since such information could only pass
from generation to generation within a family. Other
theories, such as communication with the spirit of the
deceased in a trance state, or possession, the displace-
ment of one personality by another, are even more far-
fetched. After considering all the possibilities, Stevenson
concluded that the only model that did account for the
facts was reincarnation. Although Stevenson's study is
not proof that rebirth exists, reading his careful work can
at least shake our predisposition against the belief.

The most convincing factor about past-life remem-
brances is that such recollections are so similar to
ordinary memories. If a person travels to a place where
he or she remembers having lived, it is likely that the
encounter with familiar landmarks will trigger more
detailed recollections. Moreover, many people who visit
the site of their past life exhibit behavioral traits similar
to those of the deceased person, such as relating to
relatives of the deceased in a familiar way or exhibiting
the same habits and customs as the deceased person.
Also convincing is the fact that most memories of past
lives are quite ordinary, consisting mainly of everyday
details about food, clothing, and household objects.
Although some people might recall being a Cathar or an

Egyptian princess, fantasy cannot account for the many mundane, lower-class past lives reported by people.

Accepting the Possibility of Rebirth

Once we have considered the evidence of researchers, we should take some time to discuss the idea with friends and to think about the implications of accepting the possibility of reincarnation for ourselves. Perhaps the research and reading we have done has opened us to the idea that rebirth is possible, or, at least, has convinced us to give the idea the benefit of the doubt. To help this new sense of confidence deepen into a conviction, we should return to this idea again and again. When doubts arise, instead of suppressing them, we should bring them into the open by talking to friends or by reviewing the reading and study we have done.

For instance, we may wonder why most of us cannot remember our past lives. We can answer this doubt by recalling how hard it is for us to remember the specifics of events in our childhood or even what we ate for dinner last Wednesday. Yet we do not doubt that the child we see in the photographs in our parents' album is indeed us, though we cannot remember the occasion when the photograph was taken. We might also wonder how the world population can increase, if consciousness is "recycled" rather than created anew. The answer to this question can be found by looking into the Buddha's teachings. He taught that the world we see around us is only one possible realm of existence. New human beings may be born with a consciousness from a being in another universe or with a consciousness which previously existed in an animal body.

Another way to gain confidence in the possibility of reincarnation is to read and think about the words and experiences of spiritual teachers. Accounts of the life of the Buddha, for example, tell us that on the night of his enlightenment, he saw not only all of his own past lives, but also the past and future lives of all other beings: "With His divine eye, perfectly pure and surpassing the human, the Bodhisattva [Buddha] saw sentient beings passing away and being reborn, in good castes and bad castes, good destinies and bad destinies, low and high."

But the Buddha is not the only spiritual master to have had direct experience with reincarnation. His Holiness Tenzin Gyatso, the Fourteenth Dalai Lama of Tibet, recounts in his autobiography *Freedom in Exile* how he was identified as the reincarnation of the previous Thirteenth Dalai Lama.

When he was not quite three years old, a search party looking for the new incarnation of the Dalai Lama was lead to the province of Amdo by a number of signs. The searchers noticed a house corresponding to a vision of one of the senior lamas in which there lived a small boy who recognized the leader of the search party as "Sera Lama," a Lama from the Sera Monastery. Later the boy correctly identified a walking stick, glasses, and other objects belonging to the Thirteenth Dalai Lama.

Though the Dalai Lama's story does not conclusively prove reincarnation any more than does researchers' evidence, thinking about such stories can help deepen our conviction.

8

Changing Habitual Patterns

With all the talk we hear today about alternative religions, meditation, and various spiritual paths, we might sometimes get confused about the real point of spiritual practice. Does being spiritual mean renouncing worldly pleasures and living in solitude? Does it require going into a monastery, studying religious scriptures, praying, or performing rituals? Perhaps, we might think, being spiritual means developing clairvoyance or other psychic powers through concentrated meditation.

To figure out which of these, if any, is the essence of spiritual practice, we have to look clearly and carefully at our present situation. By seeing what problems we face and what we really want and need, we can discern for ourselves a reason for engaging in spiritual practice.

We should start our analysis from the very beginning. When we look at our lives, we can be definite about at least one thing—we exist. When we look at existence more closely, we see that our life is a story or a drama which each of us perceives from an individual point of view—as *I* or the name we each call ourselves. Whatever this *I* comes into contact with, it brings into relationship with itself. Conditioned by our identification with the mind-body continuum which each of us call *I*, we relate to the world and evaluate its various objects, events, and

experiences. Because each *I* is an individual, we respond
according to individual likes and dislikes; events and
experiences are not the same to everyone—things do
make a difference. Based on our relative perspectives,
we discriminate between what is good and bad for us;
what is pleasurable, what is painful. Because each of us
experiences and judges an external world of phenomena,
we each seek those things that give us happiness and
avoid those that cause us misery. In this way, we are
constantly busy supplying and protecting ourselves.

When we look outside ourselves, though, we cannot
help but notice that the world contains billions of other
beings—humans and animals. Each being seems to be
an individual like ourselves, and thus, we reason, is
also seeking to find happiness and to avoid suffering.
Though we can recognize this commonality of purpose
intellectually, our identification is limited to our own
mind-body continuum. We cherish our own self and our
own needs more than anything else. In essence, we each
feel ourselves to be the most important being in the
universe—the one most deserving of happiness. Unfortunately, what brings one creature happiness often conflicts with the equally powerful, self-cherishing needs of
another. For this reason, beings quarrel with each other
and experience many disturbing mental attitudes. Anger,
jealousy, grasping attachment, pride, and other attitudes
that arise from self-cherishing disturb our peace of mind
and bring much trouble to the world as a whole.

Thus far our analysis has pointed out one source of
difficulty in our lives—identification with the *I*, the self-
cherishing that arises from that identification, and
the disturbing mental attitudes that self-cherishing
engenders. Because of this state of affairs, we are
constantly pushed and pulled by fears and attachments.
We often lose our balance or are swept away by powerful tides of emotion. When we think of such times in our
lives, we might recognize that eliminating them is a

good reason for engaging in spiritual practice. If spiritual practice can do anything for us, it should help us achieve greater clarity and peace of mind and reduce the number of times when we are driven by lust, rage, or other disturbing mental attitudes.

A Practical Method of Self-Development

We have never known anything other than our self-identified, self-cherishing view of the world. For this reason, the disturbing mental attitudes caused by our self-cherishing have become ingrained as habitual tendencies. In fact, what we call *personality* is really nothing more than the collection of our habitual patterns of thinking and acting. Clearly our personality is not fixed; we can and do learn, change, and grow over time. Futhermore, we can control the direction and scope of that growth through spiritual practice.

Not all of our patterns are destructive. Some are beneficial and help us relate wisely and compassionately to others. Perhaps we characteristically rejoice in the good fortune of others. Other habits are destructive and disturbing, such as becoming jealous when others receive praise or rewards. The essence of spiritual practice is becoming aware of our characteristic ways of thinking and acting. By identifying and eliminating a negative or disturbing pattern, we gain a bit more peace and freedom. By cultivating a positive or constructive habit, we enhance our ability to act in a way that helps ourselves and others.

We may think that such efforts at self-development do not have anything to do with becoming a happier person. We may blame our problems on others or on circumstances beyond our control. However, we must remember that things and experiences are not *by their nature* pleasant or unpleasant but only assume these qualities based on our attitudes toward them. It is not

necessary to change the world to make it a happier
place; we need only to make our own outlook more
positive. To avoid stepping on thorns, Tibetan teachers
tell us, we do not need to cover the whole world with
leather. Putting a pair of shoes on our own feet will do
the trick. In other words, working on ourselves is the
only practical method of improving our situation.

Once we accept that our own negative patterns are the
source of our difficulties, a question will naturally arise:
How can we work on ourselves to eliminate negative habits and to cultivate positive ones? The method
taught by spiritual teachers in the Buddhist tradition is
both simple and effective.

The first step is taking stock of our behavior. From this
basis of awareness, we can decide which habits need to
be eliminated, which changed, and which developed.
Unfortunately, this basic step is not easily accomplished.
Because we live such busy, active lives, most of us are
generally unaware of what we do and how we feel. In
many everyday situations, we fly, as it were, on
automatic pilot—making habitual responses to familiar
situations, without giving our actions or emotional
responses much thought. The way out of this dilemma
is to train ourselves in mindfulness—to learn to be aware
of what is happening in each moment. Taking a few
minutes in the evening to reflect quietly on what we
have said and done during the day is a good place to
begin. Many of the meditation instructions in Part II of
this book are also aimed at developing mindfulness.
Meditation helps us develop awareness of how we
characteristically relate to the outside world. It also helps
us begin to understand which of our actions and
thoughts lead to happiness for ourselves and others, and
which lead to pain.

As our practice of meditation or self-reflection
develops, we might discover some hidden facets of our
personality or behavior which we do not like at all. We

may be very surprised to find ourselves to be, for
example, a habitually jealous person or one given to
speaking untruthfully. At this point, it is very important
that we stay open to any newly discovered aspects of
ourselves. We should not push such realizations away,
but instead take them on as challenges to work on. Just
as rain clouds may temporarily darken the clear blue of
the sky, unwanted parts of our personality may temporarily obscure our true nature, which is in essence as
pure, clear, and bright as a cloudless sky. Although we
see our faults and shortcomings, we are, we must
recognize, okay as we are. Accepting ourselves, even
with our current problems, is an important prerequisite
to solving them.

Being gentle and compassionate with ourselves,
however, does not mean that we think we are perfect.
Rather it means recognizing that we are good enough to
be loved and cared for, good enough to possess a working basis from which we can evolve all the way to
Buddhahood. Self-hate and self-pity both create strong
blockages to spiritual progress. If we can forgive ourselves, others will not condemn us; and only if we feel
love and compassion for ourselves, can we feel these
emotions for others.

Thus far we have identified mindfulness and self-
acceptance as necessary prerequisites to changing our
patterns. These two steps alone can help us gain a little
insight and understanding. As we watch ourselves
without self-judgment, we begin to see why we are
acting as we do and the effects of our characteristic
actions. At this point, we can be a bit more analytical.
When we observe that a certain conduct disturbs us
and others, we can ask ourselves whether we want to
continue acting in this way in the future and begin to
work on eliminating the unwanted behavior.

The following example illustrates how this method
might work: When Jill's boss criticizes her work, Jill

quickly becomes irritated and angry. Often, she responds defensively without really thinking about what her boss is saying. Sometimes Jill angrily shifts the blame for her shortcoming onto a coworker. When she gets home from work on a day when she has had such an episode, Jill often criticizes her spouse or her children.

Step one for Jill is simply becoming aware of this pattern. Through her practice of mindfulness, Jill comes to recognize that her automatic anger and irritability is causing her problems at work and at home. As she reflects on her actions, Jill acknowledges that her anger at being criticized is part of her, although an unwanted part. She reflects on the causes underlying reacting in this way. For example, she may recall that when she was a child, she reacted in a similarly angry fashion to criticism from her father. She may also recognize that her self-confidence is so weak that she cannot admit a failure and that in order to keep herself up, she puts others down. This insight helps Jill understand her negative pattern. Instead of blaming herself, however, Jill determines to change.

At first, Jill simply watches herself, noting the frequency of her anger and its consequences. When she gets negative feedback at work, although she still responds in her characteristic way, Jill is more aware of how she is reacting. She cannot at first keep her irritation from rising, but she has at least become conscious of her pattern. Jill's new awareness helps her to confine her irritation to the workday and to avoid criticizing her family when she gets home. As her resolution to change her behavior strengthens, Jill begins to temper her reaction. Often, she still feels irritated inside, but she is more able to respond without defensiveness. Again and again over a period of months or years Jill works at catching herself being angry. Her goal is to get to the point of noticing when her habitual anger is about to arise. As she comes closer to this goal, Jill finds it easier and easier to control her responses and to react to critcism with patience rather than with irritation.

This example illustrates several important points. First, becoming aware of anger or another unwanted pattern *while we are experiencing it* reduces the force and strength of the negative response. The mere recognition of how we are acting begins to give us control and brings us more closely in touch with ourselves. Without this basic awareness, we have no choice but to let our habitual patterns rule our actions. Awareness creates the gap in our behavior that gives us the space to intervene and to make changes.

Secondly, the earlier we recognize anger rising or another disturbing emotion, the easier it is to derail the train of painful consequences or to stop the unwanted action in its tracks. Our goal is to learn to transform negative responses into more constructive ways of acting, until we reach a stage of spiritual development in which anger and other disturbing mental patterns do not even arise. We approach this goal in a scrics of small steps by catching ourselves earlier and earlier.

We can support our efforts to change by engaging in analytical meditation sessions (see Chapter 5), during which we contemplate the negative consequences of anger, pride, jealousy, or other disturbing patterns. We should also meditate formally on the many benefits of acting with patience, generosity, and compassion. These sessions strengthen our resolve to act positively in the future. We should recall our resolution many times during the day, especially when we are not experiencing any impulse to feel anger or another disturbing mental state. By practicing in this way, we will eventually be able to recall our resolution to act positively during the gap in our habitual pattern opened by our practice of mindfulness.

Since our personality is a collection of habits, we can slowly weaken negative behavior by working in this

systematic way. As we do so, a positive way of acting
will take the place of destructive patterns—the habit of
seeing compassionately the problems of others. Mindfulness practice helps us to be less caught up in our own
melodrama and gives us the ability to see why others act
as they do. When we become aware of our own shortcomings, we see that others have them as well. Since we
do not reject ourselves for our character defects, why
should we reject others? As our compassion and love
for other beings grow, we will find that we do not
experience troubling feelings such as anger quite so
often.

The process outlined here is not very easy. Some of
our negative habits are so deeply rooted that they are
very hard to change. The tendency to act or react in a
particular way might be a deeply ingrained habit which
we have been repeating for many, many years—maybe
even for lifetimes. Given this, the process of change can
take much time and energy. However, no activity is
more worthwhile. Once an old habit has been thrown
out and a new one integrated into our consciousness,
the new way of acting will arise as effortlessly as the
negative pattern did previously. Then we can direct our
energy toward eliminating another negative pattern,
perhaps giving ourselves a little encouragement or
reminder from time to time not to backslide.

The method described above can definitely help us
reduce our disturbing mental attitudes and the number
of negative karmic imprints we create by acting on such
attitudes. Though this method cannot eliminate shortcomings completely, it can keep such patterns under
control to the point where they cannot damage us or
others.

A similar method can help us develop our positive
qualities. As we become more mindful of such good
qualities as generosity or patience, we meditate on their
benefits and bring them to mind regularly. As we reflect

on our positive actions, we rejoice in our small successes and resolve to act even more beneficially in the future.

Perhaps this systematic approach to spiritual development sounds boring or uninteresting. It would certainly be much more exciting to solve our problems by participating in a dramatic ritual, by saying some magical mantras, or by hearing a high spiritual teacher read and expound an ancient text. There are no shortcuts, however, and no instant enlightenment. Spiritual work is a day-by-day process of slowly eliminating what is negative in our personalities and developing what is positive. It is a task each person has to undertake alone. If with dedicated effort we watch our mind and our behavior and continuously apply the method outlined here, we can transform our personality, reveal our inner beauty, and find harmony, peace, and happiness.

The interwoven Knot of Life is also called the Knot of Love.

9
Love

Hardly a day passes during which we do not hear something about love. When we turn on the radio in the morning, we probably hear someone singing about desire or a broken heart; newspaper ads tell us that people love Ma's Apple Pie or their Mercedes Benz; on the bus, we read a novel with a dramatic love story; a sign on the highway says "Jesus loves you"; our meditation teacher reminds us to love all sentient beings; our partner says "I love you" to make up after an argument.

Love, it seems, is fashionable. Love is the magic word that awakens our longings. However, when we look more closely at the ways the word *love* is used in our society, we notice that it is a very broad term, used for many different feelings. Clearly the love we may feel for a product ("I love what you do for me, Toyota!") is not the same emotion we feel for a friend; nor is it the same feeling that a religious experience might awaken. Despite this, we go on using the word love to describe every affectionate feeling: I love my sister. I love ice cream. Let's make love.

Everyone seems to know what we mean when we use love in this casual way, yet at the same time, everyone seems to experience many problems relating to love—big dramas in our relationships, loneliness, frustrations, jealousy. Perhaps we do not understand love as thoroughly as our casual use of the term indicates. Perhaps, too, we are not very adept at handling love in our everyday lives. Yet love, scientists have shown, is absolutely essential for life. An infant can die if deprived of love and affection.

The only way to solve our problems about love is to investigate the phenomenon for ourselves. To discover what love really is, we need to separate it from its connected concepts and associations. As we do so, we discover that misconceptions about love abound in three major areas: sexuality, needs and dependencies, and romantic projections.

Is It Love or Desire?

We know that love and sex are different. It is possible to make love without being in love, just as it is possible to love someone without any sexual involvement. Our confusion arises because love and sex sometimes occur together and because our lack of awareness makes it difficult sometimes to see what belongs to what.

No doubt, sexual attraction can be a strong force pulling one person toward another. Sometimes the pull is so strong we are willing to cause endless trouble and heartache for ourselves and others just to satisfy our desire. We easily misinterpret the pull of sexual desire as "being in love." But we should be clear to ourselves about why we are drawn toward connecting with someone else—whether we are addicted to the sexual sensations we experience with this partner or whether we are really in love. This does not imply that primarily sexual connections must be avoided, only that we not deceive ourselves and others by applying romantic words like *love* to all our relationships.

The ability to distinguish between sexual desire and love can be helpful in another way. A person who characteristically confuses love and desire might run from one affair to another, unable to find the warmth and closeness he or she is longing for. Each new partner brings only a little temporary excitement; then the person gets bored and moves on to the next adventure. Such a pattern leads only to more and more unhappiness and dissatisfaction.

Sexuality as a natural addition to a loving relationship, on the other hand, can enrich our lives and increase our sense of satisfaction and fulfillment. In its highest expression, sexuality leads to deep communication and a sense of genuine intimacy and connectedness. Our challenge is to be clear about our feelings and to distinguish carefully between love and desire.

Uncovering Our Needs and Dependencies

Needing someone is wanting something for ourselves; loving, on the other hand, is wanting the best for another. Needing is a self-oriented attitude, in which we want someone else to fill a gap, to make us feel less lonely, to make us feel safe and secure. Genuine love, by contrast, is being alert and attentive to someone else's needs; it is the readiness to care, give, help, and support another, with respect and an unbiased, open attitude. Most of our relationships contain some elements of both feelings.

Distinguishing between neediness and love is sometimes as difficult as distinguishing between sex and love. Our neediness often pulls us so strongly toward another person that we may think we are feeling love. But love is never pulling. On closer examination, we might find that neediness generally entails feelings of stickiness, heaviness, and difficulty, while love feels light and open and leads to a sense of joy and freedom.

Another term for this heavy, sticky, needy feeling is *attachment* (see Chapter 13). Attachment arises out of a

sense of personal insufficiency and limitation. Perhaps
we feel financially insecure, or we feel lonely and
frightened, or we are bored and want companionship,
warmth, or tenderness. Since we feel unable to fulfill
these longings ourselves, we look to help from outside.
When we meet a person who seems able to fulfill such
needs, we initially feel happy and hopeful. However,
since we want more than anything these happy and
hopeful feelings to continue, they soon change into
feelings of fearfulness, grasping, and clinging.

Attachment can range from a slight stickiness to a
heavy addiction. All attachments easily give rise to
dependency. Of course, we all have weaknesses, insufficiencies, fears, and longings, and it is natural to seek
for help in dealing with them. The problem begins when
we cling to the helper and slip into dependency. Helping
and being helped is wonderful, but we should be careful
to maintain a sense of independence. Furthermore, since
we know deep down that everything in this world is
subject to impermanence and change (see Chapter 14),
we worry constantly that whatever is giving us happiness at the moment will be lost or taken away. As a
result we are possessive and fearful and experience
many other uncomfortable mental states, such as aggres-
sion, panic, anger, and jealousy. These states may lead
to many kinds of negative actions—shouting and threats,
depression, even, in extreme cases, murder. All the
while we we may fool ourselves by saying, "I am doing
all this out of love." Of course, we are only deceiving
ourselves.

Genuine love does not *need* anybody or anything. Love
is not holding; therefore, it does not fear loss. Love is
being open and abiding fully in the moment; it is
devoted to the dynamic flow and sees the richness of
time's passage. Love neither holds to the past nor longs
for the future; rather, it is an unbiased, accepting

appreciation for what is happening right now. One who loves is aware of the truth of change and yet remains vulnerable, with the heart wide open. Only by giving a loved one all freedom can the relationship take its own shape and remain alive over time. As soon as one tries to manipulate, fix, or possess another, the flowing experience of love begins to degenerate and die.

As an example, imagine that it is a sunny day, and you are resting on the grass in a lovely garden. Suddenly a beautiful butterfly comes flying over the flowers and alights on your open hand. Because the day is warm and your palm is glittering with perspiration, the butterfly rests there, drinking the moisture. You dare not move; all your attention is focused on the butterfly, for which you experience an exquisite feeling of care. Your heart fills with joy as you observe the butterfly's delicate movements, feel the brush of its tiny feet and wings, and imagine its relish of the salty moisture on your palm. Suddenly, the wind shifts, and the butterfly flies away, disappearing into the trees. Though it is gone, your heart is still happy, knowing that the butterfly is alive in the world. You are grateful that you have had the chance to encounter such beauty so intimately. This is the experience of love without clinging.

Thus love is appreciating and respecting the natural flow, and letting things go their natural way. Love implies deep trust that there will always be enough opportunity to love somebody or something. If we really love from our own side, we are filled with warmth and happiness. We do not demand love in return, but we are delighted when love comes back to us. Our love is not a means to an end; rather, it is an end in itself.

By implication, then, love is not limited; it can embrace many. Just because we love the butterfly with the green wings, it does not mean than we cannot love the butterfly with the yellow wings or the bees or the birds. Our social conditioning often gives us the impression that we can love only one person, or at least, only one person at a time. We may live in a single, committed relationship in order to raise a family or because one person makes us happy, but we should be clear that we are doing so by choice. We ourselves might be limited, and our ability to love may not have developed to its full extent, but love itself is not limited at all. It can even extend, as the Buddha tells us, to all sentient beings.

Romantic Projections

As we have seen, we often confuse sexual attractions and feelings of neediness or dependency for love. Romantic projections are another common misapprehension about love. Often, we project, superimpose, or fantasize about a person or object and wind up believing ourselves to be in love with something that is not even there.

Sometimes it is hard for us to admit that our attraction for someone is based simply on an appreciation of his or her fine qualities and the feeling of personal well-being that results from our connection. Sometimes we cannot believe that these reasons alone account for our intense feelings, or perhaps we want our attraction to be a little more romantic. So we say to ourselves, "Yes, those qualities are part of why I love this person, but there must be something more. In addition to this person's fine qualities and what I gain through association with them, it is *the person himself or herself* that I love."

In saying this, we project an additional being or entity onto the person and then claim this projection as the cause of our tremendous love. Why are we so afraid to acknowledge that a relationship is based on a mutual exchange of beneficial qualities or on the desire to be a helpful and reliable companion? Why does there need to be a mysterious something more? Love is in essence caring for another person openly and honestly and working to bring the loved one happiness.

Moreover, we often project additional qualities on a person with whom we have a relationship—qualities that the person does not have but which we would like to encounter. When we do so, we are loving a phantom, not a real person, and we invite inevitable problems. How often, for example, are we disappointed when such a person fails to live up to our image of what he or she should be? Rather than tricking ourselves in this way, we should cultivate mindfulness and clarity about what attracts us to another person and what keeps us togther.

Another myth about love is that there is somewhere a special person, ideal for us, who we are destined to meet. Perhaps we believe that this "big love" happens only once in a lifetime, by destiny, luck, or chance. To believe this, however, is to misunderstand completely what love is. Love is not our fate, nor an external miracle, nor a mystical connection from a former life. Love is a volitional activity, an art, a skill that has to be learned, developed, and carried out. What a waste to spend our lives waiting for a big love that may never come, or to fall into despondency after a big love has ended, believing it can never be replaced.

Human beings have such a capacity that they can feel strong and intensive love toward many people in the course of a lifetime. Once we have opened to our ability to love, we need only turn toward another person with kindness and receptivity toward whatever comes and whatever will unfold.

Forms of Love

Now that we are a bit more clear about what love is, we can investigate the forms that love takes and how we deal with love ourselves.

One useful division is between unconditional love and

conditional love. *Unconditional love* is an ideal rarely
found among ordinary men and women. It is total af-
firmation and acceptance of another person; it is being
attentive and caring without expectations or wishes for
receiving anything in return. Like any ideal, unconditional love is a goal towards which we may wish to
develop, not a measure by which we should judge ourselves right now. Expecting ourselves to love in a
completely selfless manner today is expecting too much,
but aspiring to the ability to manifest such love in the
future is a rewarding and realistic outlook. In the
enlightened state, unconditional love is certainly
possible.

Most of the time, the love we experience is *conditional*—based on some condition. Though we may not
express these conditions out loud, they are implicit in
our behavior. Parents may withdraw their love when
their children act against their wishes, or they may try
to make their children feel guilty when their children
do not "repay" the parents' love with gratitude and
respect. We all do the same thing sometimes with our
friends—giving them our love and care as long as our
friends do what we like or meet our expectations. If our
friend obstructs our wishes or disappoints us, we often
turn away.

Can you imagine how much better life would be for
ourselves and others if we could let go of our conditional
minds and love without calculation or manipulation?
How much happier would we all be if we learned to
trust in the flow of life, with the confidence that all the
love we need will be provided for us by one person or
another?

Another useful way of looking at love is to divide it
into the modes of *giving* and *receiving*. Since many of us
feel a lack of love in our lives, we generally think only in
terms of how to get more love. Our consume-orientation

has trained us to seek to fill any personal gaps by external means. Thus, we treat our longing for love like our longing for, say, chocolate milk, trying to drink until we are satisfied! Receiving love can indeed feel very wonderful and is very important; nevertheless, it is only a small part of the full experience of love. When the giving mode is missing, real fulfillment in love is elusive.

A satisfying experience of love includes loving from one's own side. By itself, this form of love brings us joy and happiness. We observe that when our heart overflows with love for a tree, a flower, or a sunny afternoon, we experience a sense of openness, care, attention, and appreciation. We feel fulfilled and happy, even though the tree, the flower, or the sunny day cannot give us love in return.

When in connection with another human being, we both give and receive love, the circle is closed. In its highest expression, love is a complete form of communication, of action and reaction, of mutual giving and taking.

Opening Our Hearts

Having gained some understanding of the phenomenon of love, we can begin to develop and increase our ability to experience it. It is no use merely to long for love or to feel depressed and filled with self-pity when we are deprived of the love we need. Fulfillment in love starts when we make some effort from our own side.

It is important that we begin by loving ourselves. Loving and caring for ourselves and accepting ourselves as we are is the basis for loving others. How can we be tolerant of others if we are not compassionate towards our own shortcomings? We are on a long journey towards spiritual maturity and inner growth, and we can be happy with our progress at each level we reach along

the way. When we accept and love ourselves, we are far
more likely to open up to others without fear of
rejection.

To develop our capacity for love, it is sometimes
helpful to think of role models and examples. We can
recall what parents usually do for their children or
remember the example of other selfless people we have
met or read about. We can also think of the patience and
understanding our spiritual teacher shows to his or her
students, and we can read accounts of the great
enlightened teachers of the past, who demonstrated the
highest form of unconditional love toward their fellow
human beings. These models give us examples to
emulate and help us set the goal of developing this same
capacity for love within ourselves.

There is no quick formula for increasing our capacity to
love. We have to change our habitual patterns in small
steps, just as we work to improve every other aspect of
our personality. Our watchword in this quest should be
attention. The more we let go of our own preconceptions
and concerns, the more we open to attention and
empathy for others, the more we will be able to love.
Futhermore, we must be willing to risk hurt and
rejection. Opening the door to love means opening the
door of vulnerability. As we do so, we encourage others
to drop their protective walls as well.

Perhaps the hardest task is dropping our protection.
With honesty and straightforwardness, we must be
willing to admit our wishes and our weaknesses completely to another person. Such surrender may seem
frightening—almost like losing our identity or our self-
control. It demands tremendous trust and inner strength.
Yet love is the best way of breaking through our sense
of isolation, of reaching deeper and deeper levels of
connection with others. We can overcome our fear of
such surrender by recalling that our sense of self-

identity—like our apprehension of the identity of others
—is, in fact, an artificial projection, a comforting illusion
through which we relate to the world and its beings. As
our vision and wisdom increases, the relative boundaries
between ourselves and others will break down, and our
capacity for experiencing unconditional, universal love
will truly become limitless.

The Great Circular Banner is the flag that celebrates the victory of Buddhism.

PART II
Meditation Practice

10

Establishing a Daily Practice

Most of us spend a lot of time and energy on keeping
our bodies healthy. We avoid eating meat, shop in
health food stores, or take vitamin supplements every
day. We make sure that we get enough exercise by
working out at a health club, bicycling, or enrolling in an
aerobics or yoga class. Even those of us who do not do
anything special along these lines give our bodies a rest
each night when we go to bed. Sleep gives our bodies a
chance to recover from the hard work of the day.

But what do we do for our minds? Much of what we
feed our minds is junk food. All day long our minds are
exposed to a barrage of sensory stimulations—millions of
visual impressions, an uninterrupted stream of sounds,
all sorts of smells and tastes. Moreover, our own
thoughts and feelings as well as our myriad plans, memories, inner struggles, and confusions whirl constantly
around in our minds. Think for a moment of how many
different bits of sensory information and mental states
we have experienced today—even in the last hour. It's a
wonder that we are not overwhelmed by all the impressions the mind receives, sorts, and processes in an
ordinary day. Moreover, it is not as easy to choose what
we feed our minds as it is to select a good diet for our
bodies. We can, perhaps, choose what we read, what we

watch on television, or what movies we go to see, but we are unable to avoid the bombardment of mental impressions to which we are subjected. Nor do we often consciously exercise our minds as we do our bodies. When we were in school, we worked at training our minds to master new skills and concepts, but in the routine of ordinary life, we seldom engage in activities aimed at keeping our minds strong and flexible. Even at night, our minds do not rest completely; they simply shift into the mode of mental processing called dreaming.

Given this state of affairs, we can see that one purpose for developing a meditation practice is to give our minds a little rest —a chance to become calm and settled. Our minds can be compared to a glass of muddy water which is constantly being stirred up. When we stop stirring—for example, when we sit down in a quiet place and half-close our eyes—the mud will eventually settle to the bottom, and the water will begin to clear. Eventually, the water will become so clear we can see through it to the bottom.

This description of what happens during meditation is not just a metaphor; rather, it is the experience of thousands of meditators working in many spiritual traditions. At its simplest level, meditation gives us a chance to stop stuffing our minds with new impressions, rehashing the memories of the past, and generating plans for the future. The interval of "space" that results is more clear and orderly than the chaotic jumble of our usual mental state. It is as if our secretary has stopped throwing letters, papers, and documents on our desk for a period of time. During the interval, we have a chance to catch up on our sorting and filing. If such intervals occur often enough, we will eventually begin to see the desk top and clear it of clutter. In the same way, when we allow our minds to settle down, we create the right conditions for constructive mental activity. This calming of the mind through meditation can be called "creating space."

However, it is not easy right from the start to sit down

and just let go of all thoughts. Therefore, it may be helpful to learn to meditate by training in a preliminary practice. Meditation teachers in many spiritual traditions recommend that beginners meditate by simply observing the breath. Breathing is a natural process that is always there, dynamic and flowing even while we are at rest. In order to give the mind something to hang on to or to come back to when it starts to wander, we focus on the harmonious flow of the breath into and out of the body. This practice has a beneficial and calming influence on the mind. Bringing our mind back again and again to simply watching the breath makes it easier for us not to follow or become absorbed in other thought streams. Instructions for a meditation observing the breath are given later in this chapter.

After we have gained some familiarity with the technique of watching the breath, the next step in developing a meditation practice is to let go of our strong focus on the breath. Instead, we allow our enhanced awareness to create even more mental "space," by eliminating thoughts completely. When we need something to hold on to, we return to the breath, which remains as a backbone to steady and support our practice. As our practice deepens and strengthens, we can also work at remaining focused during breaks in our meditation sessions. For example, we can move the body and stretch the legs by doing walking meditation. Instructions for a meditation on creating space and for walking meditation are given in Chapter 11.

Once we have made some progress in creating space, we can train ourselves to increase our mindfulness by shifting our focus to various objects of observation. Chapter 12 discusses observing the body and physical sensations, both during meditation sessions and during ordinary physical activities, such as eating a meal. Chapter 13 considers methods for training in mindfulness of mental states and emotions, and Chapter 14 deals with mindfulness of thoughts and their content.

The specific exercises outlined in these chapters are
aimed at enhancing our awareness of what is happening
in the present moment. As noted, before we can change
the habitual patterns and the other automatic behaviors
which bring us so much unhappiness, we must become
aware of them and acknowledge them as parts of ourselves. As we become more conscious, more awake—the
name *Buddha* actually means "the awakened one"—we
are better able to perceive all aspects of our personality
and to discern which parts of it bring joy and contentment to ourselves and others and which parts bring us
and others problems and conflicts. Based on this clear
perception, we can begin to eliminate the negative
behaviors and develop more fully the positive ones.

Meditation Posture

In order to meditate, our body must be able to rest
comfortably while our minds remain alert. It is often
helpful to arrange a quiet place for meditation in our
house, where we can sit undisturbed for as long as we
choose. In this spot we can, if we desire, arrange an
image of the Buddha or another spiritual teacher, a vase
of flowers, and perhaps a candle and an incense burner
—objects that we will come to associate with the experience of meditation and which will help us to settle
quickly into a conducive state of mind.

Since our body and mind are so closely related, it is
also helpful to assume a physical posture which allows
us to sit comfortably during the meditation period
without causing distractions. The posture should be one
in which we are physically relaxed but at the same time
fully awake and alert. Although the details of various
postures differ, most suggest that a meditator sit upright
in a firm and stable, yet relaxed position, keeping the
back straight. The classic posture recommended by
Indian yogis has seven points:

(1) The meditator sits cross-legged on a cushion on the floor. The cushion raises the backside so that it is slightly higher than the legs. The legs can be folded into a lotus or half-lotus position to provide greater stability, but this is not essential.

(2) The back is straight.

(3) The shoulders are level, but loose. The feeling is as if the meditator were being pulled upward by a string attached to the crown of the head.

(4) The hands are placed in the lap, just below the navel. The left palm faces upward. The right hand, palm upward, lies on the left. The tips of the thumbs touch to form a circle.

(5) The eyes are closed or half-closed. The focus of the gaze of half-closed eyes is slightly downward toward a point on the floor about three feet in front of the meditator.

(6) The mouth is closed gently without any tension in the jaw.

(7) The tip of the tongue lightly touches the palate behind the front teeth.

It is less important that we follow rigidly each point of this posture than that we sit in a position that is comfortable. It is certainly possible to meditate while sitting upright in a chair, with our feet flat on the floor. In thinking about posture, we should remember that meditation is a gift we are giving ourselves, not a form of self-torture.

After assuming a good posture, we mentally glance over our bodies, relaxing any tension we find. Then we are ready to meditate.

Observing the Breath

Observing the breath should not be misunderstood as requiring forceful concentration. Rather, it is gently bringing the attention to focus lightly on the sensation

of breathing. We have all experienced such natural
concentration. For example, we may have been sitting on
a moving train reading a novel. As the story unfolded,
we became so absorbed in the characters and situations
that our actual surroundings faded or even disappeared
completely. Perhaps for a time we were not even aware
of where we were and even missed the conductor calling
out our station.

Notice in this example that we did not consciously
push away the sensation of being on the train. Instead,
we directed our attention *with interest* to the book we
were reading. As a result, our surroundings faded
naturally into the background of our awareness.

Observing the breath can be a similar experience. The
natural rhythm of our inhalation and exhalation provides
a steadying influence for the mind, which is generally
very busy. As we focus attention on the breath, distracting thoughts, fears, longings, and other emotional color-
ings gradually fall away, and our overloaded mind
becomes more quiet and clear. Perfect concentration is
a very relaxed state of mind. It is completely letting go
of anything other than our chosen object of observation.
As a result of engaging in this practice regularly, we will
feel recharged with energy and better able to cope with
our daily activities.

MEDITATION INSTRUCTION

Assume a comfortable meditation posture. Consciously
release any muscular tension. Bring your attention gently
to the breath. You may choose to focus your awareness
at the point on your upper lip where you feel the
sensation of the breath passing into and out of your
nostrils. Alternately, you may focus your attention on
the rising and falling of your abdomen with each
inhalation and exhalation.

Breath gently and naturally without consciously deepening the inhalations. Notice, with interest, whether your breathing is shallow or deep, whether and how the rhythm changes, what happens between the breaths. If your mind begins to wander, try counting in cycles of ten complete breaths, starting again with one whenever you lose count or your attention wanders.

When a distracting thought appears, focus more strongly on the breath. Ask yourself, "How is my breath at this moment? Is it deep or shallow, fast or slow, hard or easy?" Showing fresh interest in the breath as a phenomenon makes it easier to stay with it as a focus.

Another technique for dealing with distracting thoughts or sensations is to acknowledge them as soon as you become aware of them. For example, if you start to think about an unkind remark made to you yesterday, acknowledge your thought and let it go. Do not struggle to suppress the thought or try to force it away. Rather, return your focus gently to the breath and allow the thought to fade away naturally. You may need to repeat this technique many times even within a minute of meditation. No matter how often you get sidetracked, no matter how often you lose your focus on the breath, simply recognize that you have been distracted and return your focus to the breath. The technique is the same even if you suddenly realize that you have been following a train of thoughts for several minutes. As soon as you become aware that you have lost your focus on the breath, acknowledge the fact without self-judgment and return your focus gently to the breath.

If you are just starting to develop a meditation practice, or if you have practiced meditation erratically or unsuccessfully in the past, it may be helpful to keep two pieces of advice in mind. First, start with short meditation sessions. Five or ten minutes of observing the breath is a good length at the beginning. It is more beneficial to the development of a practice to get up after five minutes of meditation feeling refreshed than to force

yourself to sit for thirty minutes and to get up feeling
sore and frustrated. Secondly, try to do some practice
every day. The Tibetan word for *meditation* means
"getting used to it." Only regular practice—preferably
every day for a short time, at least—is the best way to
get used to meditation and to begin to realize its
benefits. Many meditators find that the early morning,
before you begin the activities of the day, is the best
time to practice. However, any time that works for you
and that you can stick to is fine.

Finally, try to avoid rating your meditation sessions as
good or bad. Some days observing the breath will come
easily; other days it will be quite difficult not to be
distracted. On days when you have difficulty, you can
draw satisfaction from the fact that your session has
made you aware of how busy or active your mind is on
that day. On days when you have less difficulty, be
happy about it, but do not assume that you have won
some great victory. Over time, to be sure, the overall
quality and depth of your meditations will gradually
improve. In the meantime, however, accept that
distracting thoughts are natural and that all practice is
successful in that it increases your awareness of your
mental processes.

11
Creating Space

Sometimes our meditation sessions create space for us naturally. We are able to hold our focus on the breath smoothly and easily, with relaxed yet alert attention. Other days, however, our mind is wild and turbulent; our thoughts may wander repeatedly and persistently to any object other than our meditation focus, or we feel heavy and tired and find ourselves drifting off to sleep. On especially difficult days, we may resist sitting down to meditate at all, telling ourselves we are just too busy to be bothered. What should we do to overcome these problems?

It helps a bit to remember that our difficulties in establishing a regular practice are not unique. Once long ago a student of meditation came before his spiritual master. "Master," he said, "I do not feel like meditating today. What advice can you give me?" The master thought for a moment and then replied, "If you feel like meditating, then by all means meditate. If you do not feel like meditating, then you should also meditate."

This advice, though difficult, can be very helpful. Overcoming our inner resistance and sitting down to practice even on those days when we do not feel like it at all can yield our most productive sessions. After all, meditation is really nothing more than making the effort

to understand and control the mind. Simply observing
the clatter and turmoil of an unquiet mind for a few
moments can motivate us to increase our efforts to
practice. Moreover, even on the worst days, a short
meditation session can be an oasis of relief from the
cares and concerns that make us so agitated. Meditation,
like any skill, can only be mastered with regular effort
and a bit of self-discipline. Can you imagine making any
progress in learning to play the piano if you only
practiced on days when you felt like it? Regularity has
an incredible power for transformation. Given sun,
water, and fertile soil, a seed will mature over a period
of time into a vigorous plant. If we try to watch the
plant grow, we do not observe much progress day to
day, but if we return to the plant after an absence of,
say, six months, we readily recognize how much change
has occurred.

Excitement and Dullness

Once we have overcome our resistence to practice, two
other difficulties may present themselves. Meditation
teachers describe two distracting mental states that often
occur during sessions: excitement and dullness. Excitement is usually the result of being especially busy or of
experiencing many strong sense impressions. As we try
to practice, our thoughts turn repeatedly to people we
have talked to, places we have been, or things we need
to do. This state of mind may seem very familiar. Since
we generally make no effort to control the constant whirl
of our thoughts, plans, memories, feelings, and expectations, trying to do so as we sit down to meditate may
seem an insurmountable task.

There are a number of things we can do to bring
excitement under control. First, we must recognize that
disappointment or self-condemnation will not help us at
all. After all, our mental excitement has been with us for

years, perhaps even for lifetimes. It is not so easy to change habitual patterns, but we can rejoice in the fact that we are at least making the effort to do so. Instead of becoming emotionally involved in how unstable or agitated our mind is, we should accept this mind as part of ourselves and regard our agitation with a degree of humor and detachment. We should try to bring our focus firmly to the breath and turn up the intensity of our concentration a notch to hold our attention more tightly on the object. Each time we realize that our mind is wandering, we gently but firmly bring it back to the focus, just as a kind parent takes a wandering child by the hand and leads the child back to the path.

It is also important not to follow our distracting thoughts or become involved in their content. The more energy and attention we give them, the stronger and more persistent they become. Instead, we should try to observe our distracting thoughts as if from a little distance and to regard them as clouds which will float away on their own accord, leaving the clarity of the mind unobscured. The following story can illustrate this point.

There was once a young man who wanted to learn to control his mind. He sat down and tried to let go of all thoughts, but his mind was running wild. The young man was dismayed at the turbulent nature of his mind, so he doubled his efforts. He began to force himself to concentrate harder and to push his distracting thoughts away. However, the more energy he gave to the effort, the less success he had. Finally, in despair, the young man visited a yogi who lived in a hut nearby. "What can I do to stop the distracting thoughts which disturb my meditation?" the young man asked.

The yogi thought for a moment. "There is one method," he replied quietly. "All you have to do is not think of the monkey."

The young man left the yogi's hut grateful and happy.

He returned to his house and sat down immediately to meditate. "All I have to do is not think of the monkey," he said to himself. "Just no monkey; just no monkey; just no monkey. . . ."

Soon, however, the meditator realized that as he was meditating on "just no monkey," a monkey had come into his thoughts. The harder the fellow tried not to think about the monkey, the livelier the monkey became. Soon the monkey was jumping up and down and scampering left and right.

Finally, the young man opened his eyes, and there in his house he saw not just one monkey but several. As he watched, more and more monkeys appeared. There were monkeys on the desk, monkeys on the cupboards, monkeys on the bed, and monkeys hanging from the curtains. The young man was sure he had gone crazy. In a panic, he ran out of his house toward the yogi's hut, followed by a horde of chattering monkeys.

The young man fell on his knees before the yogi. "Help me," he pleaded. "I do not mind having disturbing thoughts sometimes when I mediate, but please, please, take the monkeys away!"

The yogi laughed. "Let this be a lesson to you," he said. "The harder you try to push your thoughts away, the more persistent and annoying they will become. If you want the monkeys of the mind to go away, simply ignore them, and they will vanish on their own."

The other side of the overexcited monkey mind is mental dullness or the sinking mind. This mind too often loses the object of meditation, not through agitation but through sleepiness. Dullness can often arise when we sit down to meditate at night, when we are physically or mentally tired. In this state, our habit is that when we sit down and close our eyes, we become very relaxed and begin to fall asleep. The mind loses the edge of clarity and alertness that is necessary for meditation.

Dullness is a more serious obstacle to meditation than excitement. Sometimes we can mistakenly think that our mind is calm and settled when in fact it is sleepy or semiconscious. As soon as you realize that you have a sinking mind, you should check your posture. Make sure that your back is straight and lift the head a bit. Take several deep breaths and imagine that a fresh supply of energy and enthusiasm is entering your body with each inhalation. If the dullness persists, try turning on more lights or switch to the technique of walking meditation described later in this chapter. If none of these methods help, it may be better to end the session and take a nap. Continuing to meditate in a state of mental dullness encourages the bad habit of confusing sleepiness with relaxed but alert concentration. It may also help to experiment with meditating at a different time in the day when you are fresher and it is easier to stay alert.

It is hard not to become discouraged when one is faced with these difficulties day after day. In time and with practice, your sessions will definitely improve. Think of the persistence with which a child learns to walk. Time after time, she gets up, toddles a few steps, and falls down. Time after time, she picks herself up with infinite patience and tries again. We need to be similarly gentle and and compassionate with ourselves. We must recognize that we have been conditioned by our culture to orient ourselves toward achievement and are used to getting instant results for our efforts. In learning meditation, however, the process is as important as the goal. If we continue to push ourselves, our tension will increase, and our sessions will create stress rather than affording us release. A tree cannot be forced to grow. It must reach slowly toward the sun and bear its fruit in season.

The Buddha recommended that all tasks be approached with the attitude of ''joyous effort.'' This means that we take delight in what we are doing and engage in any activity for the joy of doing it—not with expectations of any specific results or accomplishments. Whatever comes up in our meditation, whatever happens when we sit, whatever we experience, we should not force ourselves, we should just continue.

The Creation of Space

Our everyday mind is like a workshop into which we habitually throw all kinds of rubbish and junk. The room is already filled up to the ceiling, overflowing with memories, feelings, desires, aversions, plans, and every other sort of mental impression. Still, each day we stuff in more and more. A meditation on the creation of space allows us to clear a little place in the midst of the mess. Once we have created enough room to walk around, we can begin to organize and clean up. The more order we create in the workshop, the easier it is to find the materials and tools with which we can do constructive work.

MEDITATION INSTRUCTION

Sit in a comfortable posture and consciously relax all muscular tension. Bring your awareness gently to the breath for several minutes, until you feel that any mental excitement has begun to calm down. Watch carefully for any signs of sinking or dullness, and apply appropriate counter-measures to create a state of relaxed yet alert focus.

When you are relatively free of distractions, begin to pay more attention to the outbreath in order to begin letting go of the focus on the breath. Become aware of the feeling of calmness and space that arises. Let your-self float deeper and deeper into that feeling; let the feeling of spaciousness enlarge by itself. Allow yourself to rest in the present. It is fine just to be.

When a thought appears in this space, try not to react to it or to follow it. Rather, regard it with detachment and let it disappear on its own accord. If you lose your awareness of this spacious quality, relax and gently focus on it again. Do not force your concentration. Just being quietly in the here and now is enough.

If many distractions appear, return for a time to observing the breath. When your excitement has died down, widen again into the feeling of space.

Walking Meditation

As our meditation practice strengthens, we may want to meditate for longer periods of time. However, our bodies, unused to long periods of sitting still, may make long practice difficult. Our knees hurt, our back begins to slump, or our legs fall asleep. When physical problems like these interfere without practice, it is often helpful to alternate periods of sitting with periods of walking meditation. During walking meditation, we maintain our meditative focus, but we are able to move the body and stretch the legs. Forty-five minutes of sitting meditation followed by fifteen minutes of walking meditation is a good combination.

We can also engage in walking meditation at any time. When we go out for a walk in nature, on our daily walk to the bus or train, or while walking down a corridor to an appointment, we can use this technique to create a bit of mental space and clarity.

MEDITATION INSTRUCTION

If possible, it is preferable to walk barefoot or in socks and to follow a route where you can walk in a circle or back and forth. If your hands are free, you can hold your left wrist with your right hand, hands resting on your abdomen. Walk in an upright but relaxed posture,

The Excellent Lotus Flower is the emblem of original purity.

12
Mindfulness of the Body

Calming the mind by watching the breath and creating space by letting go of all thoughts can lead to great improvements in our sense of well-being. But these techniques alone cannot solve all our problems. In order to start to work on difficult areas in our personality—enhancing its positive qualities and eliminating its negative ones—we need further inner development.

Our preliminary work has developed our ability to focus the mind and has created some mental space in which we can work—to continue our metaphor, we have sharpened the tools and cleaned the workshop. Now we can begin to look around and discover the characteristics and potentialities of the available materials and of the work space we have created. In terms of inner development, this means that, with the tool of a clear focus, we observe ourselves to see who we are, how we act, what we feel, and what we think. In other words, through meditation, we start to get to know ourselves in a way different from our normal mode of self-perception. Moreover, using the new tool of meditation, we also look at the outside world and at our external situation and begin to examine how the external environment and our inner world are interrelated.

Mindfulness is nothing more mysterious than dedicated

seeing and observing. It is being conscious and aware of what is happening in the present moment. It is seeing clearly what is really going on inside ourselves and all around us. Mindfulness helps us gain a deeper understanding of the connections between our thoughts and their manifestations in actions—between mental events and the results they produce. Through mindfulness practice, we begin to realize which of our thoughts and actions bring happiness to ourselves and others and which lead to problems and suffering. Based on this understanding, we can start to take action to reduce or eliminate unproductive habits of body, speech, and mind and to cultivate productive ones. Of necessity, such practice over time diminishes the conflicts we face and helps us become happier and more compassionate.

When we begin our practice of mindfulness, we might be suprised to discover how many of our activities we do in a half-conscious or automatic manner: We get up in the morning and eat a roll and drink a cup of coffee whether we are hungry or not. We drive to work following the same route, barely noticing the people and places we pass. When another driver cuts in front of us, we get angry and call the person an idiot or worse. Perhaps we even take these angry feelings with us to the office, where they find expression in a curt reply to a co-worker's question. When our colleague asks us what's wrong, we can't even recall what originally made us so angry. Later, immersed in the many tasks of our work-day, we suddenly experience a pang of anxiety. Did I turn off the headlights, the iron, or the stove? Where did I put my reading glasses or the bill I need to pay? Did I lock the front door? Such anxious questions demonstrate how many of our daily activities we perform in a lifeless, nearly robotic manner.

Similarly, we often take our habits and traits of personality for granted, seldom considering whether there

might be a better alternative. If we think about it, we
will probably admit readily that our personality has been
formed by the sum of all our previous life experiences:
education, relationships with family and friends, social
conditioning, and a host of other factors. We recognize
that as children, we were innocent and easily influenced;
we did not know how to discriminate and select those
experiences that would have a positive influence on our
development. But now as adults, we still often take a
childish attitude toward our problems. "I am what I
am," we say petulantly, accepting without reflection or
sense of responsibility the habitual behaviors, mental
attitudes, and value judgments that run our lives. Often,
we just follow what is comfortable and familiar, even
when we know that a particular pattern of behavior
brings suffering to us or to others.

Training in mindfulness begins with learning to focus
on particular objects of observation. Step by step, we
familiarize ourselves with techniques through which we
can observe the whole range of phenomena. We begin,
as discussed previously, with the nearest and easiest
object on which to focus—the breath. Once our ability
to concentrate begins to develop, we shift our focus to
other parts of the body and other physical sensations.
At this stage, we work to increase our awareness of our
sense impressions—touch, sound, smell, taste, and sight.
It is through these senses that the entire outer world
becomes apparent and available.

Next, we turn the bright light of mindfulness on the
functions of the mind itself. We begin by examining the
feelings—such attitudes as hatred or aversion, attraction
or clinging, and indifference. Which persons, objects, or
experiences do we fear, and which do we long for? What
causes us to have one or the other reaction to something
we encounter?

We also use mindfulness meditation to examine our

mental states and emotions. We learn to become aware
of our current mental state, whether it is happy, sad,
angry, kind, disappointed, greedy, attached, or lonely.
As we watch these mind states arise and pass away, we
learn to accept their alternation with less anxiety and to
see these passing states as merely temporary parts of
ourselves.

Finally, we use mindfulness to look at the thinking
process itself and learn to use our analytical ability to
probe the interrelation of all things and their actual
nature. Thus the techniques of mindfulness can also lead
us to realizations about such universal issues as impermanence, the unsatisfactory nature of existence within
the cycle of rebirths, and the true nature of reality.

The goal of formal meditation is to familiarize us with
the techniques and sensations of mindfulness, so that we
can eventually be as mindful between sessions as during
them. In time, we will be able to apply the same degree
of mindfulness to all our daily activities, until our
awareness is so sharpened that we remain alert and
mindful whatever we do and whatever we encounter.

Mindfulness of Physical Sensations

Some spiritual traditions teach that inner development
means shifting away from a physical orientation toward
a more spiritual approach to life. By *spiritual*, these traditions imply that a person identifies exclusively with the
mind and regards the body and its sensations as dirty or
inferior, to be denied, neglected, or ignored. Some
traditions even recommend ascetic practices, such as
fasting and self-mortification, to subjugate the body and
lessen one's dependence upon it.

However, neglecting our physical aspect can, as most
of us realize, lead to serious problems. As long as we are
in human form, our body belongs to us; it enables us to
perceive and to communicate with the outside world, to

move and to carry out all of our activities. Moreover, our body provides us with the means to read books, attend teachings, engage in meditation, and carry out all of the other activities that further our spiritual development. How can we hope to grow spiritually if the complicated organism which is our body is out of balance? Will we still feel mentally well and fit for spiritual practice if we are constantly ill?

We are learning more and more about how the mind and body interrelate and affect each other. Psychological problems often manifest in physical symptoms, and focusing on a physical problem can lead us to better understanding a psychological difficulty. Even at the simplest level, we can see the functioning of this interconnection. When we are excited or nervous, we begin to sweat; when we are embarrassed, we stammer or blush. A back problem can indicate we are trying to bear up under a psychological load that is too heavy, and a headache, that we are blocking or avoiding an issue that is crying for attention.

In our meditation on the breath, we focused on one common physical sensation. We can use the same technique to focus on any other part of the body, such as the sensation of sitting on the meditation cushion, a sense of pain or discomfort in our knees or our back, an itchy place on our skin or scalp, or a feeling of stress or tension in our jaw or neck. We can also focus our mindfulness meditation on subtler sensations, such as the beating of our heart or the sensation of our clothes touching our skin. Besides tactile sensations, we can also use as an object of focus any sound, smell, or sight within our environment, such as the sound of birds singing outside the window, the smell of coffee or incense, or the sight of a flower or an image of the Buddha. The perception of sounds, smells, and sights are physical sensations as well.

The purpose of meditations on mindfulness of physical

sensations is to become familiar with what goes on in the body. If we have been split off from our physical sensations, these meditations can help us reconnect our mental and physical functions. Moreover, by focusing on muscular tensions, we can begin to release them, and with them, often release as well the associated mental tightness that can block deep meditation. In time and with practice, the meditations described in this chapter can help us increase our awareness of the body at all times and in all activities, giving us more information about our psychological states. Such understanding improves our mental and physical health and contributes to a balance of body and mind.

MEDITATION INSTRUCTION

During each meditation session, use only one object of observation to avoid scattering your focus. If finding and holding a chosen object of observation becomes too difficult, or if the sensation you are observing disappears, focus on the breath for the remainder of the session.

Observing Coarse Physical Sensations

Relax all muscular tension and calm your mind by observing your breath. Shift your focus away from your breath to another part of your body. Choose a spot that is easy to experience, such as a sensation in your neck or your knee, the feeling of your backside pressing against the meditation cushion, or the sensation of the back of your left hand lying against your right palm. Focus all of your awareness on the spot or sensation you have chosen. Try to merge with the spot or sensation, letting go of all other thoughts and sense perceptions. Observe the sensation without labeling it as pleasant or unpleasant. Is the sensation a tightness, a burning, a stretching, a tingling, a throbbing, or some combination of these? Is it constant, or does it change over time? Keep watching the spot. When other sensations or thoughts intrude, do not follow them, but bring your awareness gently back to the focus you have chosen.

Say, for example, you have chosen to focus on a sensation in your knee. As you observe the sensation, try to remain neutral and unattached, regarding the sensation as if you were an interested witness of a phenomenon. Try not to identify with an unpleasant sensation by thinking, "I am in so much pain!" If the sensation increases in intensity, notice its increase without anxiety. Say to yourself, "It is only a physical sensation; there is no reason to panic." Try to remain calm and unmoved by what you observe. Remind yourself that the sensation you are observing is, like all other physical sensations, simply an electrochemical reaction which transmits a message to your brain. Try to watch the sensation without involvement. Perhaps, under such dispassionate observation, an unpleasant sensation will lessen or even disappear.

To take another example, say you are observing an itch on your skin. Try to refrain from scratching and instead observe it carefully. Note the buildup in muscular tension that the itch creates. If your body wants to twitch in response to the sensation, try instead to relax every muscle consciously. If the urge to scratch increases, wait another minute, and then very slowly, very consciously, move your hand to touch the spot gently to bring relief.

Follow a similar pattern for an observed muscular tension. As you focus on a stiff neck or a tightness in the jaw, allow the gentle intention build to release this tension. Softly engender a feeling of release and loose-ness in the muscle you are observing and notice how it responds. Do not generate aversion or negative self-judgment, such as saying to yourself, "If only I were in

better shape, my neck would not hurt so much.'' Be
patient with yourself, noting the way the sensation
changes over time.

Observing Subtle Physical Sensations

After you have become familiar with observing coarse
sensations, you can choose to focus on more subtle ones.
Try, for example, to become aware of your heartbeat.
Pick a spot on your body at which you can experience
the feeling most clearly, such as at the chest, on the
face, in the neck, or in the hands. Focus for a few
moments on this spot to deepen the sensation. Then
broaden your awareness along the veins and arteries
connecting this spot to your heart and feel the blood as
it is pumped through. As your concentration deepens,
you may begin to feel your heartbeat slowing down or
speeding up. You may also be able to broaden your
awareness so much that you feel your pulse simultaneously all over your body.

During another session, you may wish to focus on
your overall skin sensations. Begin to sense the feel of
your clothes against your skin—perhaps beginning with
a place of tightness or tension or one of particular soft-
ness and ease and broadening out to an awareness of
the entire surface of your body. If you are unable to find
the focus of this meditation, don't be discouraged, as
many people find this exercise more difficult.

Between meditation sessions, you should try to
remember to check and see how your body feels during
everyday activities. For instance, observe your body
during various moods or emotional states as you interact
with different people and at other times. You may be
surprised to observe that you have the habit of tensing
your jaw when you speak to a particular person or of
breathing in a flat or shallow manner when you are
anxious. Once you have become aware of these patterns,

you can take steps to relax the tension or eliminate the
habit.

Observing Other Sense Perceptions

We are generally more familar with observing sights,
sounds, smells, and tastes than we are with observing
tactile or kinesthetic sensations. Nevertheless, here, too,
we are probably not used to maintaining a steady focus.
Characteristically, our "monkey mind" jumps from one
object of perception to the next. The result is that we
perceive most sensations only superficially.

Normally we are not objective observers of the phenomena with which we come into contact. Rather, we
identify with the sense perception by making judgments
about it or by becoming personally involved. For
example, we think to ourselves, "If only I had a car,
house, dress, etc., like that one!" Such involvement
causes us to lose our clear and conscious recognition of
the object. Instead, we allow ourselves to be drowned
in the sensation of perceiving it.

To increase our ability to perceive the world around us
in a clear and unbiased manner, we can train ourselves
to observe phenomena from a little distance. During
meditation sessions, we watch without analyzing or
getting caught up in personal trains of thought. Rather,
we become a witness who simply watches what happens
and recognizes things and sensations for what they are.

Observing Forms. Choose a simple object to observe
during a meditation session, such as an autumn leaf.
With the first glance, you will see the color, shape, and
general structure of the leaf. As you look more closely,
try to notice finer variations in color and such qualities
as roughness or smoothness, symmetry, the pattern of
veins and edges, variations in thickness, suppleness or
brittleness, and any other observable characteristics. Try
not to compare the leaf to anything else or to associate

the leaf with an event or a place. Rather, attempt to appreciate the unique beauty of a particular leaf for what it is.

You might also try this meditation out of doors. Sit by a quiet pond or in the park. Choose a bird, a dog, or an insect as your object of focus. Watch the activity of the animal quietly, without judgment or projection. Take the time to really see what the animal is doing. Eventually, you may begin to develop a feeling of understanding what it would be like to inhabit an animal body.

Once you have gained some experience in keeping your mind focused, you might try sitting in the corner of a restaurant or on a bench on a busy street. From your vantage point, observe whatever happens within a small area during the course of an hour. As in other meditation exercises, when you find yourself daydreaming or losing the object of your observation, bring your mind gently back to your point of focus.

Observing Sounds. Close your eyes and let go of all other sense perceptions. What can you hear? What sounds come from afar, from nearby, from yourself? If you are sitting outside, listen to the sound of the wind in the trees. Note how the sound gets louder and then subsides.

Inside a quiet room, perhaps late at night, try listening to the silence itself. To find the object of focus, first listen intently to any small sound you hear. Sound contrasts with silence, and silence is the background against which sounds appear. Try to discern the silence by listening to the other side of sound. Another technique for identifying the object silence is to follow a sound that is going to subside—perhaps a car going by. As the sound gradually fades away, stay with it until it is completely gone. At that moment, you have found silence. Once you have a clear idea of the object silence, you will be able to "hear" it and focus on it even when there are noises around.

Another exercise is to practice conscious listening within a group or when you are conversing with a friend. Make an effort to stop thinking about what the speaker will say next and how you will reply. Instead, really listen to what is being said to you without judging what you hear or projecting yourself or your ideas into what the other person is saying. See how much more you hear when you are giving another person your undivided and sympathetic attention.

Observing Smells. Focus on a particular smell—a lighted stick of incense, a fresh flower, or a ripe piece of fruit. Let go of other perceptions and focus on the smell to recognize its full character and intensity. Is the smell sharp or sweet, strong or faint? What effect does perceiving the smell have on your body or on your emotions?

Particularly in springtime it can be marvelous to take a walk in nature and observe the world of odors. Try to respond to what you observe without aversion or cling-ing. Allow each smell to be what it is. A "bad smell" is only a sense perception. Remind yourself that such judgments are imposed by the social norms of a partic-ular society, rather than being inherent in the smell itself.

Observing Tastes. You can do this meditation whenever you are eating. Try to make the whole meal a medita-tion. Arrange everything on the table and sit down. Do not start to eat immediately. Wait until your mind is settled, and remind yourself that your intention is to eat with mindfulness in order to make your body strong and healthy.

When your mind is focused, take your fork and place a bite of food into your mouth. Put down the fork and chew the food carefully and thoroughly. Focus on the sensations on your tongue, teeth, and throat as you swallow. Only when you have experienced the full sensation of one bite should you pick up your fork to take another. Savoring each bite in this manner will probably make you satsified with eating less, and your enjoyment of what you do eat may also increase.

Watch to see what arises in your mind as you eat. Are you, for example, already thinking about a second portion before you have finished your first? Do you continue to eat after your stomach is full? Try consciously to let go of all the emotions and associations that you have connected with food over the course of your life. Instead, strive to experience the sensation of eating with fresh wonder and appreciation.

13

Mindfulness of Attitudes and Emotional States

Finding the object of focus for mindfulness meditations on the body is relatively easy. We can readily discern the parts of our physical form and the phenomena our senses detect in the external world. Locating the object of mindfulness in meditations on attitudes and emotional states, however, is more difficult. The first step is to define what we are looking for. In this context, *attitudes* refers to the faculty of discrimination by which we determine our basic feeling toward something we encounter or experience. In general, our habitual pattern is to categorize our attitude toward any object, person, or experience as one of *attraction,* one of *aversion,* or one of *indifference.* An *emotional state,* on the other hand, is a pervasive response, such as joy, sadness, jealousy, anger, resentment, and the like. An emotional state can arise as a result of a basic attitude. For example, attraction for one person can lead to jealousy toward others. Using meditation to become aware of our basic attitudes and emotional states can give us important information about ourselves and our patterns, leading to greater balance and stability.

Uncovering Our Basic Attitudes

Everthing we encounter in life gives rise to a feeling of
like, dislike, or neutrality. Conscious or unconscious, this
perception is always there. This reaction is triggered by
our placing what we perceive into relationship with ourselves. Based on our previous experiences and conditioning, we determine whether a thing is good for us—likely
to be helpful or to bring us pleasure—or bad for us—
likely to lead to suffering. Those things or experiences
which seem neither pleasurable nor harmful give rise to
a neutral or indifferent attitude.

These basic attitudes motivate many of our actions and
reactions. If something has given us pleasure in the past,
we try to hold on to it or to meet it again. If something
has caused us discomfort in the past, we try to avoid it
or get rid of it. Thus much of our striving and struggling
takes place because of our likes and dislikes and the
attitudes of attachment and aversion that arise as a
result. Sometimes we can be successful at managing and
manipulating to make the world the way we would like.
All too often, however, we cannot. Moreover, since
everything in the world is subject to change, even those
pleasurable things we have managed to come close to
cannot be kept forever; nor can we prevent conditions
and factors from arising which bring us into contact with
unpleasant or painful experiences.

A few simple examples can make this point more clear.
Let's say that we have to go on a long business trip and
leave our lover or partner behind. Because we are
attached to the person at home, we are sometimes not
able to appreciate the many new people we meet, the
landscapes we travel through, or the fine food we eat
along the way. We act in this way because our attachment has caused us to overestimate the good qualities
of one person at the expense of all other people and
experiences. Moreover, our attachment causes us to
forget all of the problems and difficulties we might have

had with our lover or partner in the past—even the times when we longed for an interval of privacy and separation. Thus attachment is an unrealistic attitude that often distorts our perceptions.

The same mechanism operates when we are attached to an object or experience. When a treasured possession is lost or broken, we are sometimes so miserable that we lose the ability to appreciate and enjoy life. In our exaggerated response, it often seems as if our ability to be happy is tied directly to this one thing.

This is not to say that we should not feel affection for our family and friends and that we should not enjoy having nice things. When we allow our happiness and peace of mind to be bound up with things that are by their nature impermanent and transitory, however, we are setting ourselves up for inevitably suffering in the future. Moreover, we must be careful to distinguish between attachment and love. *Love* is the desire to make another person happy; it is an attitude which is focused more on the other person than on ourselves. *Attachment*, on the other hand, exaggerates the good qualites of a person or object and seeks to draw the object or person closer to ourselves and not to be separated from it. Attachment is distorting and disturbing; it leads inevitably to possessiveness, selfishness, and clinging.

Aversion is a similarly disturbing attitude. When we experience aversion, we exaggerate the harmful qualities of a person or object as they relate to ourselves. Aversion leads to irritation, anger, annoyance, resentment, and many other negative emotional states. For example, say that a neighbor complains about the music we like to play. As we listen to the neighbor's words, irritation rises, which quickly turns to anger. We answer back sharply, and soon the exchange becomes a heated shouting match. We see ourselves as an innocent victim of an unprovoked attack. The many favors the neighbor has done in the past are forgotten. They are replaced by images of every thoughtless or annoying thing the

neighbor has done. A relationship that had been characterized by friendliness and cooperation has, because of
the exaggerated response of aversion, become one of
conflict and pain.

Strong feelings of attachment and aversion thus are the
causes of much of our suffering. An alternative to this
pattern is cultivating an attitude that regards the things,
people, and experiences of the world in a detached and
realistic manner. Such an attitude can be called *equanimity*. Equanimity does not imply that we are apathetic.
Rather, it is a balanced state of mind that makes us
flexible and able to cope with whatever situation we
encounter. If circumstances require us to leave something we like, we can let go without excessive feelings of
pain and loss. If, on the other hand, circumstances force
us to encounter something we dislike, we can maintain
control and not be overtaken by anger or depression.
Thus equanimity is the skill to let go and to accept. This
gives a kind of freedom. In the absence of attachment
and aversion, we are free to make choices and to act in
the most compassionate and helpful way in a given
situation.

The following story illustrates the advantages of equanimity: Once in China, in a small village near a river,
there lived a wise old man. One day, the village farmers
digging in a field uncovered a chest full of gold. The
people of the village were overjoyed, proudly proclaim-
ing themselves to be the luckiest people in the world.
They put away their farming tools and prepared to live a
life of ease. Each night, they held a feast to celebrate
their good fortune. Everyone in the village attended,
except the old man. He alone was unmoved by the
excitement in the village. He preferred to keep to his
daily routine and observed the jubilation around him
with a half-smile.

Robbers had heard of the good luck of the villagers.
One night while everyone was sleeping, they entered the

village and made off with the gold and with the food the
villagers had in storage. The next day, the villagers were
distrought. They cried and wailed, calling themselves the
most unlucky people in the world. Only the old man
was unmoved. With a half-smile he reminded the villagers that they had lived through famine and hard
times before and could certainly do so again.

News of the misfortune which had overtaken the
village reached the king. He took pity on the villagers
and sent them seven boatloads of grain and other
foodstuffs. Once again, the villagers were overjoyed.
Because of the king's gift, they neglected their field work
again and lived on the king's food. Only the old man
went about his daily routine, watching the villagers with
his characteristic half-smile. At harvest time, only the old
man had crops to bring in. When the food the king had
given the village was used up, the old man shared his
small harvest with the villagers and listened to their
complaints with a half-smile.

Cultivating an attitude of equanimity, like the one
practiced by the old man in this story, makes it easier to
cope with the inevitable ups and downs of life's circumstances. The old man knew that the one thing the
villagers could count on was change. The same thing
that is a cause of happiness today may be a cause of
misfortune tomorrow. Equanimity—an attitude free of
attachment and aversion—allows us to keep our balance
and our sense of perspective. It takes into consideration
the fact that people change, that feelings and thoughts
change, that situations change. It allows us to maintain
our equilibrium in the face of these changes, and to
see people, objects, and events for what they are.

MEDITATION INSTRUCTION

Choose an object, a situation, or a person to be the focus
of your meditation for this session. Allow your mind to

create a vivid image of the chosen focus, alive in all its detail. As you contemplate the image, allow your feelings to arise, and note carefully the attitude you experience. Try not to judge or repress a negative or aversive response, or to compare your actual response to what you think you *should* be feeling. Rather, note and accept whatever attitude you recognize as authentic without evaluating it.

Once you have recognized clearly your current attitude toward your object of focus, ask yourself questions such as the following to investigate this attitude more closely: Have you always held this attitude toward this person, object, or experience? What circumstances or events led to the formation of this attitude? What circumstances or events could cause this attitude to change? How would you feel if you were separated from this person, object, or experience? What body sensations or other physical reactions do you note as you ask and answer these questions?

As your understanding of your current attitude deepens, try to cultivate an attitude of detachment and equanimity. Remind yourself that your current attitude is just a snapshot of where you are today, and that attitudes, like everything else in this world, are subject to change over time.

As you end your session, resolve to use the understanding you have gained to increase your mindfulness of your attitudes toward the people, things, and experiences you encounter in your everyday life. When you catch yourself experiencing strong attachment or aversion, note its effect on you. Remind yourself of the advantages of cultivating detachment and equanimity.

Mindfulness of Emotional States

Emotional states are those pervasive states of mind, such as joy, sadness, jealousy, anger, resentment, excitement, pride, and depression, that we experience as a result of life situations. Sometimes emotional states arise from basic attitudes of attachment or aversion—for example, we are more likely to be irritated by criticism from someone we dislike. We can also become attached to or experience aversion for an emotional state itself. For example, we might be attached to feelings of anticipation or seek to avoid feelings of anger.

Emotions are not in themselves problematic. The problems begin when we identify with a particular state ("I am sad" instead of "There is sadness"). By identifying with an emotion, we risk being drowned or swallowed up by an emotion that assumes unrealistically large dimensions. Emotions also cause problems when we distort our own perception of our feelings—selecting emotions we find admirable and encouraging them to arise, while repressing emotions we want to avoid. In doing so, we not only reject a part of our own reality but also create tensions that can subtly manipulate our moods and behavior.

Mindfulness of emotional states helps us to recognize our unwanted emotions. Sometimes, this mere recognition helps us get control of our emotions and frees us from their compelling influence. By practicing mindfulness, we can learn to open up to all sorrows and joys— to whatever is happening in our lives. To go beyond unwanted emotions, we have to go through them, which implies opening to them, facing them, and accepting them. Eventually, we will find that our whole emotional drama will get smaller and more manageable. We may even begin to find positive aspects in previously rejected parts of ourselves.

Thus, one prerequisite to changing ourselves is acknowledging our emotional states and accepting what we experience with a caring and loving attitude. How can we expect to cultivate compassion for others if we are not able to feel compassion for ourselves? How can

we be patient and forgiving of others if we do not
extend these feelings to ourselves? Mindfulness implies
that we say yes to ourselves, with all our emotional
problems and weaknesses. This does not mean that we
stop trying to change those aspects of ourselves that
bring suffering to ourselves and others—just that we
become aware of and accept where we are, as a basis for
growth and change.

In this context, it is useful to think of the example of
the woodcarver. One day, while walking through the
forest, the woodcarver found an uprooted oak-tree
stump. Though the stump was clotted with dirt and
matted with moss and trailing vines, the woodcarver
could see in the stump the shape of his next sculpture.
As he wrapped the stump carefully in a blanket and
loaded it into his cart to carry home, he pictured in his
mind the beautiful carving that would emerge from the
stump in time. To the woodcarver, the stump was
precious and delightful because despite the dirt, he
recognized the fine quality of the wood and its potential
for becoming a wonderful piece of art.

We can look at ourselves in the same manner. We
know our emotional nature is far from perfect. We
realize that we often experience extreme or distorted
perceptions that lead to unhappiness and confusion.
However, like the woodcarver, we know that our human
form has the potential for great accomplishment. All of
the the great enlightened beings of the past, including
the Buddha, began with similar raw material, with
similar imperfections and faults. With self-acceptance
as a starting point and with a fearless determination to
become more conscious and aware, we can definitely
improve and develop. As long as we shut ourselves off
from our own emotional nature, as long as we escape
from our pains and fears into a world of illusions and
fantasies, we will stay caught in an emotional web of our

own weaving. When we train ourselves to be mindful of our emotional states as they arise and practice fearless acceptance of whatever we experience, we create the causes for increased happiness and peace of mind.

MEDITATION INSTRUCTION

Shift your awareness to your emotional state. What are you experiencing at this moment? Are you happy, sad, enthusiastic, upset, fearful? Examine this state carefully and allow it to be what it is. Try to watch the state as an observer, without identifying yourself personally with the emotional condition. If the state you identify is pleasant, try not to hang on to it; if it is frightening or painful, do not try to push it away; if it does not fit into your self-image, do not deny or repress it. Accept whatever state of mind you discern as a part of yourself.

Dealing with Sadness. If the emotional state you are experiencing is sad, disappointed, or depressed, use the opportunity to take a close look at this emotion. Try to enter your sadness more deeply and to feel it in its full intensity. Do not wallow in the experience of sadness; rather, investigate the state and observe its effect on you. Where in your body do you experience your sadness? What mental pictures or associations does your sadness give rise to? If you find yourself falling into negative self-judgment, tell yourself that sadness, like all other emotional states, is nothing more than a natural energy that arises in the mind. It is a part of life. Accepted without resistance, sadness and depression will definitely fade away in time. Remind yourself of how many emotional states you have experienced in the past. Ask yourself where these states are now. Recognize that sadness, depression, and all other emotional states are transitory. If, after a while, you find yourself feeling heavier and more sad, try to counterbalance your sad-

ness by shifting your focus to an experience that has
made you very happy. Remind yourself that sadness is
only one of many possible emotional states.

Dealing with Fear. If the emotional state you are feeling
is fearful, concentrate on relaxing all muscular tightness
or tension. When you are more relaxed, turn openly to
your fear while maintaining the position of an objective
observer. Do not try to push the fear away or build walls
and defenses against it. Allow yourself to face your fear
and look at it squarely. Is it still so frightening? Remind
yourself that fear is a projection into the future. The
present moment is still bearable. Ask yourself questions
such as the following to investigate your fear: When did
the fear arise? What caused the fear? What physical
sensations accompany the fear? What mental pictures or
associations does the fear give rise to? Are these associations realistic? How is your fear related to your attachments and aversions? Acknowledge that fear is a transitory mental state. Generate a feeling of happiness that
you have at least been able to become mindful of your
fear and accept it as a natural part of your emotional
makeup.

14
Mindfulness of the Content of Thoughts

For purposes of mindfulness training, we can divide the range of possible perceptions into four categories, three of which have been covered in previous chapters: our body and the physical world, our attitudes of attraction and aversion, and our emotional states. The fourth category, which is discussed below, is the content of thoughts. This category includes all the mental functions which do not fall into one of the other three divisions, including thoughts, sequences of thoughts, the process of thinking, the mind itself, and any abstract ideas such as theories, philosophies, or truths.

Mindfulness of thoughts can begin with the simple practice of observing how frequently thoughts appear. Increasing our awareness of how slowly or quickly our thoughts change gives us useful information about our mental state. For example, slow changes may indicate a calm and peaceful state of mind while rapidly changing thoughts that jump from one thing to the next probably indicate that we are restless, excited, or nervous.

If, in addition to the frequency of our thoughts, we also become mindful of their content, we can learn even more about ourselves. Let's say, for example, that a red sports car pops frequently into our mind. We picture ourselves driving it and attracting the envy and admira-

tion of everyone who sees us. Generally such favorite
daydreams pass through our consciousness virtually
unnoticed. However, as we watch our mind during
mindfulness meditation and become aware of such
thought-pictures, we can take the time to figure out their
meaning. As we reflect on such thoughts, perhaps we
recognize, for example, that we desire luxurious or
prestigious possessions to make up for some imagined
personal inadequancy or shortcoming.

Meditation on the content of thoughts can also give us
the time to examine the attitudes and emotional states
that accompany our thoughts. Such awareness helps us
understand our habitual patterns—what we characteristically long for or worry about. We can use the insights
thus gained to further our personal growth.

In our busy and active lives, we seldom take the time
just to watch our mental processes. We are used to
having a thought and immediately identifying with it
or acting on it. During mindfulness meditation, however,
we adopt the position of an observer and use part of our
mind to witness in a detached manner our thoughts and
their content. As we do so, we observe how easily we
are swept away by the mental melodramas we create for
ourselves and how readily we are caught up in actions
and events without real reflection.

Observing our thoughts without identification can be
compared to watching, say, the people and activities in
a supermarket from a glass-enclosed manager's office
located above the shopping floor. From our observation
post, we see a young mother rushing to complete her
shopping while comforting a crying infant and an elderly
couple comparing brands to find the least expensive can
of tuna. However, though we perceive clearly the
people, events, and transactions taking place below us,
we do not judge or evaluate them in relation to ourselves. Our stance is one of objectivity and little ego-

involvement with the drama on the other side of the glass.

Our normal position, on the other hand, is more like being a shopper in the market ourselves. We are always selecting, bargaining for the best price, subjectively involved in choosing what we want for ourselves, what is good for us, what we feel about this or that product or event. Quite often, the result of such immersion is that our objective awareness falls away, and our automatic, habitual patterns take over.

The goal of mindfulness meditation on the content of thoughts is to cultivate a middle ground between these two positions. By becoming aware of our own mental processes, we can train ourselves to remain aware of the stream of thoughts while simultaneously participating fully in the events of our life. Actually, this is not such a major change as it might seem. Our subconscious mind records far more events, sensations, and feelings than we do with our conscious awareness. Mindfulness meditation simply brings this subconscious awareness to a clear and conscious level. Doing so allows us to be more fully connected to our thoughts and to act on them and react to them with full awareness.

How is this possible? Say we are conversing with someone. As the conversation progresses, we dedicate one part of our mind to observing our selves and our surroundings while the rest of our mind engages in the conversation as usual. This observing part of our mind gives us objective information and feedback about our actions and reactions. For example, it notes the tone of our voice, our facial expressions and gestures, the attitudes, emotional states, and mental associations triggered by what is being said. Such increased awareness allows us to monitor our own behavior, giving us the opportunity to make decisions, to change our actions or our attitudes, and to temper our emotional responses.

Conscious recognition tends to increase conscious control, letting us decide what we say and do, rather than being driven by our habitual patterns.

MEDITATION INSTRUCTION

Awareness of the Frequency of Thoughts. Focus on the breath to calm your mind. Then let go of the breath as an object and focus on the spaciousness of mind. As thoughts arise into this clear space, note how often new thoughts appear within a set period of time, such as five minutes. A thought can be a mental picture, a remembered remark, an internal comment or sensation, or anything else that appears on the blank screen of the mind. Try not to follow each thought as it appears; rather, allow the thought to fade away and wait for the next thought or impression to arise. Compare the frequency of thoughts during several meditation sessions over a period of days or weeks to assess how calm or busy your mind is under different conditions.

Awareness of the Content of Thoughts. Focus your calm mind on the content of your thoughts as they arise. Remain in the position of an observer, who witnesses each thought as it comes up, notes its content, and lets it go. Cultivate the relaxed feeling of lying on the grass on a summer day looking up at the sky. As each thought passes through your field of vision like a cloud, watch it with detachment, noticing its shape and size, without becoming emotionally involved. If you do not nourish thoughts by participating in their story, they will soon fade away. Be aware of any thoughts that recur repeatedly. Ask yourself how these thoughts indicate your present mental condition.

Awareness of the Mind Itself. Another meditation in this category is observing our mental functions themselves to see where thoughts come from and against what kind of background they appear. This meditation is focused on the nature of mind itself, which is a state of clarity and knowing. It demonstrates that your mind is like the clear blue of the summer sky. Though it can be obscured temporarily by clouds, such obscurations do not affect its underlying clarity.

Quiet your mind and wait for a thought to appear. After the thought fades away, focus your awareness on the background against which the thought appeared. Alternatively, if your mind is very busy, observe a thought from its beginning to its end. Try to become aware of the gap between the end of one thought and the beginning of another. Try to widen that gap and abide within it. In that space, you are in touch with the nature of the mind itself.

You may have difficulty finding the focus for this meditation. We are seldom without thoughts or without the internal dialogue of the observer-part of our mind, which comments on what is going on. Moreover, it is easy to confuse sleepiness or dullness with a clean, thought-free mind. The focus we are seeking is a state of crystal-clear, fully awake awareness, without thoughts. Even if our meditation yields only a brief glimpse of such a state, the experience may be enough to convince us that behind the parade of our thoughts is the mere ability or potential of knowing and being conscious. The mind itself is this potential; only by the various thoughts and impressions of consciousness does the mind become colored and take shape.

Mindfulness of Concepts and Ideas

Mindfulness of the content of thoughts also includes the observation of concepts, ideas, theories, and beliefs. Any idea that can be contemplated, analyzed, or expressed can be examined by this method. Often our understand-

ing of an idea such as rebirth, impermanence, or suffering is merely intellectual. We can use the techniques
of mindfulness meditation to gain a deeper and more
integrated understanding of such an idea. Using mindfulness meditation to work with a concept such as
impermanence or suffering has two parts. During
meditation sessions, we take the concept as our focus,
concentrating on it single-pointedly to examine it from all
angles. Between sessions, we use one part of our mind
to watch how the concept reveals itself in the situations
and events we encounter. This two-pronged method
helps us gain a clearer understanding and a firmer
conviction about concepts important to our development.

Investigating Impermanence and Uncertainty

One topic that mindfulness meditation can help us
understand is impermanence. The first step is to think
clearly about the concept with the aim of strengthening
and deepening our intellectual understanding. Then
when we carry our mindfulness of this issue out into our
daily lives, we begin to see countless examples and illustrations of the principle of impermanence in things we
observe and encounter. These examples, in turn, can be
incorporated into our meditation sessions on the topic.

When we focus our awareness on impermanence, the
first thing we may notice is the pervasiveness of the
human drive for constancy. Laws and regulations, con-
ventions and traditions, historical monuments and sky-
scrapers are all signs of the human drive to hold on to
the past, to keep things the way we know them, to give
ourselves a sense of security.

In our daily lives as well, we may realize, we have our
fixed routines and our well-organized plans, all of which
are designed to prevent the unexpected. We strive so
much for control because we are afraid we will not be

able to cope, afraid that something will arise that will
reveal how vulnerable and dependent we are. When we
are mindful of our underlying emotions, we may also
become aware of how helpless we feel against the laws
of time, the certainty of change and decay, and the
inevitability of our own death. When we are mindful
and quiet, we realize that impermanence threatens us.

As we contemplate further, we may realize that many
of the activities of society are motivated by our uneasi-
ness about the future. We construct buildings of concrete
and steel, develop technological means of conserving our
resources, and conduct research into cures for disease
and disability in an attempt to make the world steady,
solid, and durable. This facade of external protection
makes us believe that the structure of our lives is lasting.
Such seeming solidity helps us to repress, push down,
and cover up our fear of change. Thus we find upon
observation that we have developed the habit of pretending that we can keep things static, that we can know
what lies ahead. This habit leads us to project permanence onto everything—material things, persons,
situations, even ideas.

As our mindfulness of the issue of impermanence
deepens, we may realize how many of our actions are
predicated on our belief that things will stay the same.
For example, when we leave the house in the morning,
we are certain that we will find it in the same condition
when we come back in the evening. Similarly, when we
park our car in a lot, we fully expect it to be in the same
spot when we return in a few hours.

More significantly, when we talk to a friend, we take
for granted that he or she is still the same person we
knew previously. We also project permanence onto our
relationship with our lover or partner, picturing in our
minds our still being together next week, next month,
next year—forever. When we become aware of this

pattern, we should remind ourselves that holding on to the past obstructs the beauty of maturation and growth. In this world, fixity is synonymous with death.

As for ourselves, no matter how our appearance or ideas have changed, our conviction is that we are still ourselves, possessing essentially the same identity as we did at every previous stage of our lives. Instead of seeing our multidimensional personality with its constant change, we often limit ourselves to a single, narrow self-image, which we make solid and frozen, thus taking away any possibility of improvement.

As we contemplate further, we may discover that we have predicated our actions on a false belief in living forever. No one, not even a person suffering from a serious illness, thinks he or she will not be here tomorrow. Rationally, of course, we know that death is certain, but in practice, we act as if we will live another forty or sixty years—if not forever. Facing the real uncertainty of life simply seems too overwhelming, too frightening.

Becoming mindful of this pattern of denying impermanence may eventually lead us to a realization: Though we project permanence to make ourselves feel more secure, deep down our sense of safety is very weak. Actually, our conscious mind is just pretending to feel secure, while at the subconscious level, we know that our own lives and everything around us is uncertain. This deeper level of knowing sometimes pushes through into consciousness. Though we try to push it down, we discover that we have only been tricking ourselves. Since the reality of decay and death is in conflict with our pretended state of safety, it is inevitable that we clash again and again with the true situation. These clashes cause confusion, frustration, and all sorts of emotional difficulties. This line of reasoning may lead us to the conclusion that we would have far fewer problems if we

would learn to face up to our fear of impermanence,
learn to live with it, and, by so doing, overcome it.

To open ourselves to impermanence and uncertainty
means acknowledging consciously and accepting the fact
that everything—including ourselves—is subject to
constant change. The seemingly solid and immovable
things of this world, as modern physics continues to
remind us, are actually processes. Every moment things
disintegrate, evolve, transform themselves, become new.
As we sit in meditation and mindfully ponder this fact,
myriad examples may come into our minds—mountains
crumbling slowly to the sea, flowers blooming and
withering, snakes shedding their skin, our own bodies
changing as we age.

Such thoughts, however, do not need to be depress-
ing. Change also brings the possiblity of renewal.
Accepting this fact is letting go of comforting illusions
and learning to live fully in the present. If we respond to
joyful situations by holding on to them while they are
taking place and then go over them again and again, like
running a film in our minds, our attention is withdrawn
from what is happening to us right now. Letting go of
the past leaves us open, receptive, and able to appreciate
and experience present events in their full intensity.
Similarly, projecting into the future and picturing in our
minds exactly how we want things to be blocks the
natural unfolding of events. Clinging to a future dream,
like holding on to past events, is living in a dream world
of our own fabrication. A stance of openness often gives
us the opportunity to connect with outcomes far better
than those we planned or projected.

The aim of the great spiritual masters of the past has
been the development of equanimity. *Equanimity*, the
balanced perspective from which we view the world
without attachment or aversion, also implies that we live
fully in the present moment without attachment for past

events and without aversion for outcomes other than
what we planned. Such a stance allows us to embrace
the pleasant parts of our lives and to transform the difficult parts into opportunities for growth and development. Our contemplation of the truth of impermanence
can convince us that even our most intractable habitual
patterns can be eliminated by our changing the causes
and conditions that have given rise to them. In the same
manner, we can cultivate new, more positive habits and
qualities.

Thus meditating mindfully on impermanence can
inspire our spiritual practice. Since everything changes,
we, too, can change. There is no limit to what we can
do! Even full enlightenment is possible for us. As the
great Indian philosopher Nagarjuna said, ''Since everything is impermanent, everything is possible.''

MEDITATION INSTRUCTION

Quiet your mind and turn your focus to the topic of
impermanence. Bring to mind things you have read
or heard about this topic, including the ideas in this
chapter. Try to develop a clear mental picture of impermanence and its effect on you. As you continue to
meditate, dedicate one part of your mind to the position
of observer. The observer-part of your mind watches to
make sure that the rest of your mind does not wander
off the topic. It also follows the stream of thought of
your contemplation, noting the physical responses that
arise, the attitudes of attraction and aversion engendered
by various thoughts, and the emotional responses you
experience as you ponder the topic.

As your intellectual understanding deepens, allow your
mind to search for confirmation of the truth of impermanence in the events and situations of your daily life. At
this stage, a part of your mind holds on to the idea of

impermanence while the rest of your mind investigates various objects and experiences to see whether and how they manifest this characteristic. For example, you might bring to mind a longtime friend, a treasured possession, your own physical appearance, checking to see whether and how each illustrates the principle of impermanence. Between formal meditation sessions, cultivate awareness of impermanence in your daily life to discover how impermanence applies to various new situations and to gain immediate and fresh experiences that deepen your inner conviction.

The Vase of Great Treasures contains spiritual jewels.

15
Selflessness

To stop the samsaric melodrama in which we exist once and for all, we need the realization of selflessness or, as this key Buddhist idea is also called, emptiness. We have seen that our disturbed mental attitudes, such as anger, jealousy, attachment, and so forth, take away our peace of mind. These attitudes are the real troublemakers in our lives. Though we can certainly reduce the extent to which these negative mind states control our behavior by working on our personality and increasing our mindfulness, in order to eliminate them completely, we have to end our false way of seeing reality.

Previous chapters have explored many of the projections, denials, and other mistaken perceptions which build up the drama of our lives. In essence, these misperceptions have their root in a basic fallacy. Because we identify with an *I*, our relationship with the world is dualistic. In other words, we perceive that we are "over here," while the world of others is "out there." Our complete identification with the mind-body combination which we call *I* or *me* creates a feeling of separation and limitation. Since we are split off from the rest of the world, we react to things outside ourselves with fear, helplessness, and a sense of overwhelming insecurity. All our projections, fantasies, and mistaken perceptions are attempts to cover up this fear, to create a sense of artificial security and to fill us with the hope that we can still get what we long for. However, such illusions also distort reality and keep us locked into a self-fabricated world, which is out of touch with the true nature of reality.

Our identification with an *I* also contributes to our bewilderment by encouraging us to discriminate between things we like and things we do not like. Our determination of liking, or attachment, for some person, thing, or experience is, as we have seen, based on the perception that this person, thing, or experience can give *me* pleasure. We feel aversion, on the other hand, for those things that cause *me* pain. Our disturbed mental attitudes that exaggerate the goodness or badness of phenomena are, thus, based on an attitude that cherishes the self—the *I*—more than all others.

As long as we identify with an *I*, we cannot have an objective view of the world. Instead, we evaluate whatever we come into contact with and place it into relation with ourselves. Thus all of our perceptions are tainted by our previous conditioning, our life experiences, and our subjective judgments. Only when we are able to go beyond the relativity of our self-centered view can we begin to perceive the true nature of ourselves and other phenomena.

How, we might ask, can we ever go beyond a subjective view? After all, we certainly seem to be permanent, independent, partless entities who exist in the world by their own power and whose subjectivity is thus inevitable. However, Buddhism teaches that this seemingly self-evident, independently existing self is an illusion. How can this be? Surely, we exist. There is someone here who is reading this book, who talks, listens, eats, sleeps, loves, and gets angry. Buddhism does not dispute the existence of this functional self. In fact, the teachings warn us against falling into the extreme position of *nihilism*—the view which denies any objective truth or existence. The point is rather that the *I* does not exist in the way we perceive it—as an entity that exists inherently, from its own side. The perception of an independent, concrete, solidly existing *I* is an illusion which we superimpose on the self that does exist—that relative self that eats, sleeps, reads, and meditates.

Let us explore this superimposed *I* more fully. Bring to mind the sense of self that we experience when we are relaxed. Then compare this sense of self to that which we would experience if someone ran up to us on the street and shouted, "Stop, thief. You took my wallet!" At these words, we would think, "He said that to *ME!*" and a strong and solid sense of *I* would arise—a self at which anyone could point a finger. If we observe this strong sense of *I* carefully, we see that it seems to be an additional entity or being that sits inside our body. This entity is neither our body nor our mind, but rather the possessor of the body and the perceiver of our mental functions. This *I* seems to be the controller and the authority behind everything we do and everything we call *me* and *mine*.

But when we begin to look for this independent, concretely existing *I*, we discover paradoxically that it is hard to find. Logically, if this *I* exists as it appears to—as an autonomous entity—it must exist within the mind-body combination or apart from it. There is no third choice. If the *I* exists as part of the mind-body combination, we should be able to locate it. So, we ask ourselves, is the *I* contained in my arm, my leg, my torso? If my legs are cut off, does the *I* get smaller? Perhaps, we think, the *I* is in the cells, the DNA, the atoms of the body. However, if this is so, wouldn't each strand of hair on our head necessarily contain the *I*?

If the *I* is not in the body, we might reason, perhaps it

is in the mind. Is the *I* my emotions, my thoughts, my consciousness? But since the mind, as we have seen, is a constantly changing stream of thoughts and feelings, which of these is the *I*? Is the *I* a happy thought? Is it an angry thought? Is it a sleeping consciousness or a waking one? And if the *I* is located neither in the body nor in the mind, is there any other place to look apart from the body and the mind?

Analyzing the situation in this way may lead us to the conclusion that the *I* which we perceive at times so strongly is a fabrication—a projection, like all the others, the purpose of which is to make us feel more safe and secure. Moreover, just as we superimpose an inherently existing self on our person, we do so on all the phenomena of the world. These, too, we make to seem concrete, solid, self-existent. *Selflessness* or *emptiness,* Buddhism teaches, is nothing more mysterious than the realization that phenomena and persons—including ourselves—are empty of the fantasized projections we impose on them.

Since persons and phenomena do not exist in the way we conventionally perceive them, in what way do they exist? Buddhism teaches that the existence of persons and phenomena depends on causes and conditions. Thus our body exists in dependence upon our arms, legs, torso, cells, DNA, atoms, and all other parts of our physical self, and our mind exists in dependence on the thoughts, feelings, and sensations which make up our consciousness. Thus the *I* is merely a name that has been imputed upon one particular combination of mind and body, just as the name *table, house,* or *car* is a name imputed upon a particular combination of wood, metal, plastic, and glass parts that make up one of these phenomena.

Ignorance about the true nature of existence is the cause for our bewilderment and our disturbed mental attitudes, which propel us into engaging in confused activities. The result is our ongoing samsaric melodrama. When we recognize that our ego-oriented perception of the world is mistaken and that objects and situations are not the way we perceive them, we come closer to the ability to see things as they are. When we are able to see ourselves and the world as free from the false qualities we project onto them, we move closer to the state of joy and harmony the Buddhists call *nirvana*.

MEDITATION INSTRUCTION

As a preliminary to the meditation on selflessness, first identify the fantasy self that you will negate through meditation. This fantasy self is the sense of *I* that is the doer of deeds, the thinker of thoughts, and the controller of all that belongs to *me* and *mine*. One way to pinpoint this self is to think of the *I* that looks out through your eyes or the inner entity that perceives the sound that enters through your ears.

To identify this self, try in everyday situations to cultivate mindfulness of the sense of self that arises when you are in a threatening situation. When this solid and tangible sense of self arises, try to get a clear mental concept of it. Once you have a clear idea of how this sense appears, you can begin to look for it in formal meditation sessions.

Begin your meditation by calming your mind. Then recall an experience in which you were very excited, upset, or frightened. Recollect the situation in vivid detail. Observe the *I* that arises. Do not at this point try to analyze or investigate this *I*, since doing so might cause the big sense of *I* to diminish. Simply observe it carefully to build up a clear perception of it. When your sense of the *I* is clear, ascertain its characteristic appearance. Do you see it as a train of thoughts or as the actual thinker? Does it seem to be the same *I* that

appears at other times or in other situations? Does this
I seem to consist of parts or does it have concrete,
independent self-existence?

When you think you have a clear image of the *I*, try to
find it. Search among all the components of your body—
eyes, feet, heart, blood vessels, fingers, nerves—and
among all the components of your consciousness—
thoughts, memories, feelings, sensations. Can the *I* be
found in either place? Use your reason to investigate
the mystery fully. For example: If the *I* is my body,
would the *I* be diminished if part of my body were cut
off? And, if the *I* is my thoughts, is it an angry thought,
a loving thought, a jealous thought? Ask yourself
further, if the *I* is neither in my body nor my mind,
how could I say "my hand" or "I feel bad"?

Do not fall into the error of thinking that because the
I is neither the body nor the mind, it does not exist. We
do exist conventionally—just not in the way in which we
generally experience ourselves. Recall now this
conventionally existing *I*—the *I* that goes shopping and
watches television, the *I* that experiences joy and pain.
Can you see that this *I* arises in dependence upon your
particular combination of the body and the mind, onto
which the name *John* or *Jane* or *I myself* is imputed? Can
you see that there is no thinker behind the thoughts, but
merely thinking? Try to recognize that this conventional
I is sufficient for all the activities of your daily life, and
that no *super-I* is necessary in order for the self to
function.

As you conclude your meditation session, resolve to
use the insights you have gained to cut through the
attachment or aversion you experience for people,
objects, and situations that seem able to provide happiness or to produce pain *from their own side*. Recall that
such perceptions are an illusion, and that everything is
fluid and ever changing. As a result, there is nothing
solid to grasp or to avoid—and no *I* to do so.

Observing the Predominant Object

The four categories of mindfulness we have discussed—namely, observing the body, attitudes, emotional states, and thoughts—include all possible perceptions and experiences we may encounter. By training in mindfulness of each category, we learn to distinguish between different objects of perception, thus sharpening and deepening our awareness. The final step, which is also the ongoing practice of mindfulness meditation, is using this heightened awareness to become conscious and mindful of whatever object our mind is perceiving in the present moment.

Training ourselves in awareness during formal meditation sessions teaches us to recognize what occupies our mind. Too often, as we have seen, we live our lives according to some external schedule or set of demands. Living up to others' expectations, we neglect our own needs. Mindfulness training puts us more closely in touch with ourselves and gives us the space to listen internally and become aware of our current inner condition. When we are open and relaxed, we may find that unwanted fears or other negative mind states dissipate of their own accord.

Mindfulness of whatever object of perception arises is called *observing the predominant object*. It is the heart of mindfulness training. During meditation sessions on the predominant object, we give ourselves the freedom of moving from focus to focus, depending on what arises and on what feels appropriate and beneficial. This increased flexibility allows us to deal with whatever appears to our mind both during and between meditation sessions.

The principle idea is that we reserve a bit of time each day to look within. As we do so, we remain open and receptive to whatever comes up and accept it as part of ourselves. Thus, we deepen our awareness of what is

going on in our conscious mind as well as the perceptions recorded and processed in deeper levels of our
personality. Just as keeping a journal keeps us in touch
with what we have been doing, so a formal meditation
session on observing the predominant object allows us to
stay conscious of what is happening inside. By training
ourselves in this way, we increase our conscious awareness during the activities of everyday life. Based on this
awareness, our wisdom will grow, enabling us to be
more fully present to ourselves and to the world.

MEDITATION INSTRUCTION

Relax your body and bring your attention to the breath.
Then gently let go of the breath and expand your
awareness to a wider range of perceptions. Remain
within the here and now, including receptivity to your
physical sensations, attitudes, emotional states, and
thoughts. Maintain an attitude of openness, letting
things happen, letting physical and mental events arise
and pass away. Your position should be as an observer
who watches from a little distance, not fully involved in
what you perceive.

   If you observe that your mind repeatedly encounters
the same thought or impression, make it your focus of
mindfulness. Use the same techniques for examining this
thought practiced during previous meditation sessions.
Once you have chosen a focus, stay with it for the rest
of the session. Jumping from one object to another can
make you feel restless. Observe the object you have
chosen as predominant from several angles. How is it
experienced in your mind? Does it also find expression
in your body? What associations do you make with it,
such as mental pictures, sounds, emotions? As you stay
focused on the object, watch to see if your experience
of the object changes. If after some time the object dis-

appears, return to watching your breath, which remains the backbone of your mindfulness practice.

When you have gained some experience in this type of meditation, you can try being even more flexible. Rather than remaining focused on one predominant object during your meditation session, allow your attention to follow the various objects that come up in your mind. Try to remain mindful and balanced so that you neither jump from one impression to the next nor hold tightly to one particular sense impression, emotional state, or thought. If you choose to remain with one impression for a period of time, do so. If you choose instead to follow the flow of impressions as they come and go, that is also fine. The point is that you direct your concentration and focus it where it feels best.

If nothing particular arises as a focus, try letting go of everything. Go deeper and deeper into yourself, experiencing the vast openness, the calmness, the peace. Feel how the waves of thought subside and sink below the moving surface into the stillness of the innermost mind. Keep your awareness clear. Correct the mental disturbances of excitement and dullness as soon as you recognize them. Remain fully in the present moment.

Appendix

RESULTS OF A SURVEY

The following responses were gathered during informal interviews with American dharma students during the summer of 1990.

Question: *What were your motives for looking into spirituality?*

• Hearing about, reading a biography, or meeting an advanced spiritual person; being inspired by his or her accomplishments.
• Encountering a teaching that seems true and relevant, answers open questions, and provides a means of practical progress.
• Having glimpses of altered states of consciousness, including drug experiences and ESP; wanting to experience similar or deeper experiences.
• Feeling an inner urge to seek the truth, discover the meaning of life, or find out what comes after death.
• Noticing that spiritual people, such as those in organized dharma groups or monks and nuns, cope better with life.
• Looking for methods to become a better person.
• Feeling the need for guidance by a teacher.
• Seeing the limitations of materialistic approaches to finding happiness, such as alternative lifestyles, therapy, etc.

• Realizing that one's present life situation, including career, partner, or family did not bring real satisfaction; wanting something better.
• Searching for help with serious life problems.
• Experiencing good feelings and a sense of benefit when participating in spiritual ceremonies, rituals, meditation, chanting, etc.
• Seeing the shortcomings and contradictions of one's familial religion; looking for better explanations of metaphysical issues.
• Seeking answers to existential questions, such as suffering and pervasive dissatisfaction.
• Rebelling against the narrowness of society and seeking freedom; wanting to be rid of one's limitations and insufficiencies.
• Wanting to have a direct experience of the mystic dimension.
• Experiencing a life crisis, such as a serious illness or the death of a friend or relative.
• Feeling that one is drowning in misery or despair.

Question: *What factors supported your initial approach to spiritual practice?*

• Reading accessible teachings and biographies.
• Experiencing helpful behavior within a spiritual group.
• Feeling accepted within the group or from the teacher, whatever one's background, previous beliefs, or lifestyle.
• Hearing simple, basic teachings which help in daily life.
• Being allowed to participate in the activities of a spiritual group with no pressure to "convert."
• Meeting other Westerners who practice an Eastern religion; seeing that they can integrate it, that it works for them, and that they can communicate their experiences easily.
• Starting with simple practices, such as mindfulness of

breathing, body sensations, emotional states, and
thoughts; learning about the Four Noble Truths.
• Practicing in the Zen style of just sitting down and
observing one's mind.
• Doing Hatha Yoga exercises to relax and bring the body
and mind to the here and now.
• Experiencing the help that meditation brings to daily
life.
• Practicing meditation in a group.
• Having access to a personal meditation teacher/advisor
to get help with problems and to direct one's purpose.
• Arranging a small altar; performing some practice or
ritual daily.
• Seeing that the teacher and other students live normal
Western lives and that they are not "exotic aliens."
• Being able to ask questions during teaching sessions
and to discuss problems at the moment when they arise.
• Not feeling proselytized; not feeling pushed or
manipulated; having the freedom to leave the group for
a time when necessary.
• Having no obligations; not feeling pressured to
contribute money; attending teachings that are free or
inexpensive.
• Being in a group with a hierarchy and without
"insiders."
• Having fun with group members; meeting, sharing
social life.
• Finding that group members are open and accepting
of all spiritual traditions.
• Being able to get advice but not being told what to do.

Question: *What blocks or obstacles made your approach to
spiritual practice difficult?*

• Having to practice on one's own.
• Lacking sufficient support to build up the discipline
necessary to continue.

• Lacking enough information to see the relevance and purpose of meditation.

• Feeling overwhelmed by the vastness and complexity of Tibetan Buddhism; lacking practical information about paths and methods.

• Finding it difficult to visualize while meditating.

• Putting too much pressure on oneself to study or practice.

• Engaging in prolonged sitting meditations too quickly.

• Feeling resistance to having to pray and chant in the Tibetan language.

• Resisting exotic cultural elements; feeling that one does not want to become a Tibetan or adopt foreign habits.

• Performing rituals and practices without sufficient explanation as to their purpose and how they work.

• Lacking self-confidence; feeling stiff, blocked, or incapable.

• Having difficulty integrating practice with one's everyday life or closing the gap between the meditation session and the rest of the day.

• Experiencing frustration with the slowness of the process or with one's lack of immediate results.

• Feeling guilty for adopting a new religion.

• Feeling discouraged by how much one's mind wanders during meditation.

• Finding recitation of mantras or prayers boring or meaningless.

• Fearing that analytical meditation is a form of brainwashing.

• Feeling suspicious and fearful about the secrecy requirement attached to some teachings.

• Experiencing resistance to having a living teacher; feeling that devotion to universal or impersonal forces is easier.

Recommended Reading

Batchelor, Stephen. *Alone With Others: An Existential Approach to Buddhism*. New York: Grove Weidenfeld, 1983.

Chodron, Thubten. *Open Heart, Clear Mind*. Ithaca, NY: Snow Lion, 1990.

Dalai Lama. *Kindness, Clarity, and Insight*. Ithaca, NY: Snow Lion, 1984.

Dass, Ram, and Stephen Levine. *Grist for the Mill*. Berkeley, CA: Celestial Arts, 1987.

Dass, Ram, and Paul Gorman. *How Can I Help? Stories and Reflections on Service*. Oakland, CA: LC Publishing Co., 1985.

Goldstein, J. *The Experience of Insight: A Simple and Direct Guide to Buddhist Meditation*. Boston: Shambhala, 1987.

Goldstein, J., and J. Kornfield. *Seeking the Heart of Wisdom: The Path of Insight Meditation*. Boston: Shambhala, 1987.

Lhalungpa, Lobsang. *The Life of Milarepa*. Boston: Shambhala, 1977.

McDonald, Kathleen. *How to Meditate: A Practical Guide*. London: Wisdom, 1984.

Nalanda translation committee. *The Life of Marpa the Translator*. Boston: Shambhala, 1986.

Rabten, Geshe, and Geshe Dhargyey. *Advice from a Spiritual Friend*. Revised edition edited and translated from Tibetan by Brian Beresford. London: Wisdom, 1984.

Rabten, Geshe. *The Essential Nectar*. Edited and translated from Tibetan by Martin Willson. London: Wisdom, 1984.

Stevenson, Ian. *Twenty Cases Suggestive of Reincarnation.* Second revised and enlarged edition. Charlottesville, VA: University Press of Virginia, 1980.

Trungpa, Chogyam. *Cutting Through Spiritual Materialism.* Boston: Shambhala, 1973.

Trungpa, Chogyam. *Meditation in Action.* Boston: Shambhala, 1974.

Trungpa, Chogyam. *Myth of Freedom.* Boston: Shambhala, 1976.

Tulku, Tarthang. *Gesture of Balance: A Guide to Awareness.* Berkeley: Dharma Publishers, 1976.

Tulku, Tarthang. *Knowledge of Freedom: Time to Change.* Berkeley: Dharma Publishers, 1985.

Willson, Martin. *Rebirth and the Western Buddhist.* London: Wisdom, 1974.

QUEST BOOKS
are published by
The Theosophical Society in America,
Wheaton, Illinois 60189-0270,
a branch of a world organization
dedicated to the promotion of brotherhood and
the encouragement of the study of religion,
philosophy, and science, to the end that man may
better understand himself and his place in
the universe. The Society stands for complete
freedom of individual search and belief.